Beginner's Guide To Oriental Rugs

Beginner's Guide to Oriental Rugs

by
Linda Kline

ROSS BOOKS

P.O.BOX 4340
BERKELEY, CALIF.
94704

Photos

Maps of Rug Producers

Kline, Linda, 1944-
    A Beginner's Guide to Oriental Rugs.
        Bibliography: p.
        Includes index.
        1. Rugs, Oriental. I. Title.
NK2808.k54   746.7'5   79-21014
ISBN 0-89496-002-9
ISBN 0-89496-012-1 pbk.

Introduction

As a long time collector of Oriental rugs, I am frequently asked for advice. Although there are numerous books about Oriental rugs on the market, many people come to me and say they feel unenlightened after reading most of them. The books, they say, are usually poorly organized, difficult to use and marginally helpful.

After reflecting on various books and discussing them with a variety of knowledgeable, professional friends of mine (both Oriental rug dealers and professors), the reason for this discomfort became very clear. There has long been a need for a book with the beginner or student of Oriental rugs in mind. That is, a book that gives not only a description of how rugs are made and a short history of them, but a book that gives some systematic method that the reader can use to go about identifying rugs.

Further discussion made it clear that the most sensible way to classify Oriental rugs is by the motif or design in the rug. Hence, although a modern rug may be made in Pakistan, if the motif is Turkoman you would point out that it is a Turkoman style made in Pakistan (just as you may say that the porch of your house has Greek columns made in England). If you know what kind of rugs various villages and tribes make, you can further refine your knowledge about your rug. You may then be saying your rug has a Turkoman motif of the Yomud tribe although made in Pakistan (this is comparable to saying the porch of your house has Greek Corinthian columns made in England).

Therefore, I have arranged this book in two major sections. The first section lists, with very clear illustrations, many of the most common motifs found in Oriental rugs. Along with the motif is a description of the major areas that produce that motif. The second section of the book lists the major rug producers catagorized by geographic area.

The method, then, is to identify the motif in your rug first. Next, you can look at the various villages or tribes that produce that type of motif. Under each village or tribe is a description of the type of weave (ie. kind of knot used, size of rugs, etc.) that the villages or tribes produce. Using this method, you can better decide if your Turkoman rug was indeed made by the Yomud tribe.

Frequently, especially with very recent rugs, you will find dealers making conflicting statements as to "what kind of rug this is". Usually, it is because they don't know for sure themselves. In modern times, everybody copies everybody else's motifs. This, however, does not detract from the enjoyment, the beauty, or the value of the rug (just as knowing that your Greek Corinthian columns were made in England would not detract from the enjoyment of the art itself, the enjoyment of its durability, and the enjoyment of its financial appreciation over time).

A good glossary, index, and clear introductory chapters have been added to help you become acquainted with the wonderful, enjoyable and very rewarding world of Oriental rugs.

Linda Kline
La Honda &
Palo Alto, Calif.
Fall '79

Table of Contents

Motif Illustrations

History & Making of Oriental Rugs

The earliest appearance of the loom in history was about 3000 B.C. when it was already known and widely used in Egypt. Its roots, therefore, are lost in antiquity.

earliest record

Obviously, none of the Oriental carpets from the times of the ancient pharaohs are in existence today. The oldest known rugs, in fact, were discovered in 1949 by the Russian archeologists Rudenko and Grjansov in the Siberian valley of Pazyruck high in the Altari mountains. They found the tomb of some Scythian chiefs. The frozen graves were around 2,500 years old. Two carpets were among the items in the grave, and they are now in the Leningrad museum. One carpet is about 4x6 meters (about 13x20 feet) and made of felt. The other is knotted and about 1.5x1.8 meters (about 5x6 feet).

museum rugs

Other than a few very rare exceptions, like these frozen carpets, there are no carpets in existence from before 1300 A.D. There are some fragments of carpets in museums dating from the period 1300 to 1500. Starting around 1500, we begin to find existing carpets. The average person, however, would be fortunate to run across anything from the early 1800s.

tribal motifs

Since villages and tribes, in centuries past, were isolated with little communication, compared to today, it is expected that patterns varied greatly from one area to another. Tribes, towns and areas could be easily and clearly identified by their distinctive colors and motifs.

synthetic dyes

As time moved to the present, some major changes occured. Synthetic dyes were introduced in the mid 1800's and, in recent times, machine instead of hand-made carpets have shown a dramatic increase. The advent of machine-made carpets, along with the higher standard of living brought on by the oil industry, has resulted in dramatic changes in the production of hand-made carpets.

tradition

Even today, however, in countless villages throughout the East, families continue to make carpets just as their forefathers did in centuries gone past. Here is how a typical hand-made carpet is constructed:

First, a loom is erected. In its simplest form it is just a few poles:

loom

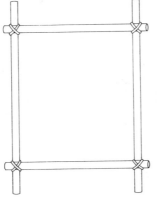

Strands of spun wool or thread are then strung taut from top to bottom. These threads are called the warp. The further apart and thicker the threads are, the coarser the final rug is.

warp

weft

Suppose we number the strands in order from left to right. The next step for the weaver is to gather all the even numbered threads and pull them toward him. He then passes a shuttle carrying another wool thread (called the weft) across the loom from left to right between the odd and even threads. The weft threads are then beaten down tight. By doing this pattern over and over, one gets a carpet consisting of warp (vertical) and weft (horizontal) threads.

kelims

By simply varying the color of the weft threads and varying how many warp threads the weft threads go over and under in a given pass, you can produce varying designs. Carpets made this way are called kelims.

The kelim technique has limitations and weaknesses. Round or curved shapes are very difficult to produce. Also, long straight lines are difficult to produce because too long a gap cannot be left in the fabric without weaking it. The result is a rug usually dominated by long lines which are somewhat wavy and broken (see color section example).

weakness

Carpet weavers of long ago found a way around these problems. They would set up their loom with warp threads and run a few weft threads through. They would then take very short pieces of colored thread and go across the loom tying them to the warp threads. The knots would be tied so that the frayed ends of the thread faced the weaver. After that is done, the weaver would then run a few weft threads through and beat everything down tight.

knots

The weaver would then have the strength of a good kelim, the added strength of knots, and ability to do almost any design. In addition to all this, you would have the ends of the short wool thread, called the pile, facing the weaver and giving the carpet a nice feel. There are two major kinds of knots found in Oriental carpets. One is the Turkish knot or Ghiordes knot. The other is the Persian knot or Senneh knot. A third, less used and desired, knot is the Jufi knot. The following illustrations show how the three are tied.

different knots

Turkish Knot

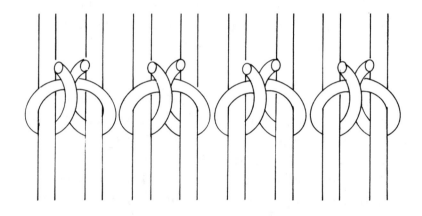

Ghiordes knot

The Turkish knot, also known as the Ghiordes knot, is used in many rug types, and is not exclusive to Turkish products alone. When inspecting a rug, the Turkish knot will have pairs of threads forming the pile, but so will one of the less desirable Jufi knot forms. Close inspection of both sides of a rug will reveal what knot form was used. Since the Turkish knot is wound around one warp thread, and the Jufi knots are tied around two, it is fairly easy to distinguish between the two.

Jufi knots

Persian Knot

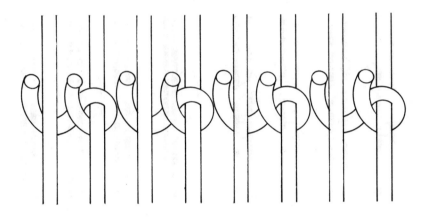

The Persian knot is alternatively called the Senneh, named after the Persian town. But, as is true for the Turkish knot, this style of knotting is used in rugs originating from other countries as well as some from Iran. The Turkoman rugs, some Caucasian and Turkish rugs, are also woven with the Persian knot. As can be seen from the illustration, the threads are wound around two separate warp threads, and the ends are pulled up on either the right or the left of the warp. The nap of rugs woven with this type of knot will separate individually, whereas the threads separate in pairs in rugs woven with the Turkish knot.

*Senneh
knot*

Identification

Jufi Knots

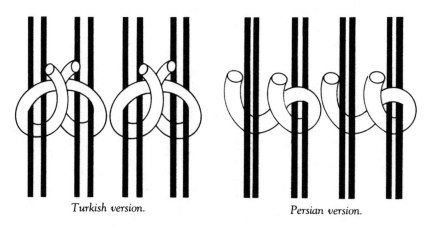

Turkish version.   *Persian version.*

Two knot forms

The illustration above shows both forms of the Jufi knot. The knots are essentially the same as the Persian and the Turkish, except that two warp threads are incorporated in each knot. The Jufi knots are considered to be inferior, as are the rugs produced with the knot. Since only half the number of knots are required, the rugs can be made much more rapidly than those using the Persian or Turkish knots, and only half the amount of wool is needed.

The techniques of weaving have changed very little over thousands of years although, in modern times, synthetic dyes and new loom styles have been introduced. With modernization, quality has been sacrificed in some areas for the sake of production.

Tradition

A nomad studio.

Choosing Your Rug

When considering the purchase of an Oriental rug there are a few guidelines which help in making a wise choice. Since there are many factors that influence the value of a given rug, it is important to remember the steps of its manufacture. With this understanding, better choices can then be made, and possibly a costly mistake avoided.

purchasing a rug

As we have mentioned, Oriental carpets are woven on looms. Obviously, the size of the carpet is dependent on the loom. Rigid looms, also called horizontal looms, are those used by most nomadic tribes. The rugs produced on these are limited to the height and width of the loom, usually no longer than seven feet. Adjustable looms, with rollers to accommodate the long warp threads on one end and the finished sections on the other, are adapted to much larger sizes. Generally, the rugs produced in the "factories" where many weavers work on one carpet, and where adjustable looms are used, are the only sources of room-sized carpets.

looms

rug factories

natural dyes

Oriental carpets are produced from yarn dyed with either natural or synthetic dyes. The natural dyes are made from plant and animal sources, which have been processed to produce the desired hues. Synthetic dyes are chemically manufactured and are available prepackaged, thereby saving months of preparation otherwise required.

color range

Generally, specific types of carpets are available in a limited range of colors or combinations of colors. This is not an absolute standard, however it is something to consider when purchasing a carpet. For example, if pastel tones are desired, the varieties of carpets available are limited to a few Persian and Chinese rugs and some Indian reproductions. Likewise if red tones are required, the choice is vast including almost every variety of Turkoman, Caucasian and Persian carpet.

wools

Carpets have varying textures resulting from: the foundation threads (warp and woof), the knots (type and number per square inch), length of pile, and the type of wool used in manufacture. An excellent carpet need not have an extremely tight weave, long or short pile, or finely spun threads. Each distinct type of carpet has its own characteristics that lend it its particular qualities. For example, Kirman rugs have been traditionally associated with their soft, lustrous wool, whereas Hamadan carpets are produced from coarser fibers which are somewhat dull by

carpet wear

comparison. These distinct features lend themselves to certain kinds of wear. It is important to consider this factor of wear before purchasing a carpet for particular use. If the chosen carpet is to be used in a high traffic area, a hallway for instance, one of the more durable rugs would be best.

Designs range from simple, geometric forms to extremely ornate floral and animal motifs. Historically, designs used in rug manufacture were associated with either specific areas of production or with the tribe that produced the carpet. These motifs were, more or less, the trademark of a given rug type. Thus, with most old carpets and many of the ones still made today, one can identify the carpet through design and physical characteristics. We can only discuss the origin of the design in many modern machine-made carpets, but modern carpets are just as durable and rewarding as the old ones.

design features

Rugs are finished on the sides and the ends. The sides are most commonly overcast with yarn or selvaged. Overcast sides are bound with yarn the full length of the rug. This protects the foundation threads from wear. Selvaged sides are produced by weaving the warp and woof threads together on the outer edges of the carpet. End finishings include web (selvage), fringe, and a combination of the two.

overcast or selvaged sides

Rug finishings should be inspected to make sure they are secure. If the ends are wearing, or the side finishing is not secure, the carpet will eventually begin to unravel. Carpets used in entry halls and positioned under doors where they are constantly rubbed will tend to wear most readily

careful inspection

*proper
maintenance*

on the edges and ends. This type of damage can be prevented by proper maintenance. If a rug begins to wear, have it repaired immediately. To prevent uneven wear, periodically rearrange the rug, and always keep a mat under it.

*wool
quality*

The quality of wool contributes to the value and durability of a rug. It can be stiff or supple, fine or thick, but most of all it should be strong and resilient. Brittle wool, or moth-damaged areas, can totally destroy a carpet's value and eventually its usefulness. Because these problems are not always readily apparent, it is very helpful to inspect a carpet under a magnifying glass. Try pulling some of the fibers under magnification to test their resilience; they

spin

should not break readily. The spin of the wool can also be checked at the same time. Properly spun wool is strong and the individual threads that form the yarn should be securely bound together to withstand wear.

*knot
forms*

There are primarily two basic knot forms used in Persian, Turkoman, Caucasian, Chinese and Indian carpets. The two most common knot forms are the Senneh or Persian knot and the Ghiordes or Turkish knot. To determine the type of knot used, one method is to separate the nap threads of the carpet. If the threads appear in pairs, the Turkish knot has most likely been used.

Knots per square inch is a term frequently used, often as a

gauge to a rug's quality. The number of knots per square inch determines the density of wool, and the more wool, the more durable a carpet will be. Tightly woven carpets are generally speaking, the most durable and the most expensive.

knots per square inch

Wool rugs are subject to moth damage which can be extremely destructive to a carpet. It is often difficult to notice, therefore carpets should be checked very carefully. Moth larvae will embed themselves either under the carpet or deep in its pile. The damage will result in a weakened foundation (which is the most expensive to repair) or in the nap, where the yarn is eaten away and the knots eventually pull out. Larvae perfer areas that are dark and undisturbed such as a corner area under furnishings. These spots should be checked, and with rotation of the rug, most damage can be prevented. New or used rugs purchased from reputable dealers will most likely be free of infestation. New rugs are treated with insecticides before importation and once in a dealer's shop they are frequently moved around.

moth damage

Oriental carpets generally have some irregularities in shape. Most new carpets are fairly symmetrical, but each has its own characteristic features. This is especially true of the nomadic carpets that are woven on small looms. If the warp threads are not evenly spaced, or more knots are incorporated in some rows than in others, the resulting carpet will be uneven. This feature can reduce the value of a carpet, depending on how extreme the variations are. It

irregularities in shape

is true that some of the most highly-valued carpets are irregular, but these rugs are prized for their antique value. For modern rugs, extreme irregularity is not a prized feature.

blocking

Some carpets are woven very tightly, and these rugs tend to curl at the edge. The more loosely knotted rugs can even have rippled edges. These features can be corrected. Blocking a carpet will usually remedy such problems, but if this does not work, hand sewn threads can serve to ease together rippled edges or flatten out curled ones.

nap features

Some carpets have a closely cropped nap, others have a longer pile. The length of the nap is not a conclusive indicator of a rug's durability. Some of the finest Oriental carpets have naps clipped to one half inch or less. It is far more important to inspect the carpet's knots, the wool and the foundation threads in order to determine its durability characteristics.

One final remark should be made here regarding place of purchase. Established rug dealers (including mail order houses), rug auctions, estate and garage sales comprise the major sources of Oriental rug purchases. Established dealers, with rugs on display, as well as large mail order houses, are recommended as the most reliable sources for two reasons. It is generally the practice that dealers will allow you to take a rug on approval and, if for some reason it proves unsuitable, the rug may be returned or exchanged.

Also, because rugs appreciate in value over the years, many dealers will accept one of their own (old) rugs in part payment (or in exchange) for a new, more expensive one. If you wish to make such an arrangement, the matter should be discussed prior to purchase, and established in writing on the sales slip if at all possible.

Rug auctions, estate and garage sales seldom offer guarantees. Traveling auctions, usually advertising in local newspapers, have thrived for many years, but the consensus seems to be that their success is due more to buyers' ignorance than to any evidence of bargain purchases. Once the item is purchased at auctions, no refunds or exchanges are offered. Estate and garage sales have similar hazards, but if one is experienced and knowledgeable, a worthwhile investment can be had. In any case, the old adage of "buyer beware" most certainly applies to any Oriental rug purchase. The investment is significant and some caution is of great value.

auctions

rug
classification

Oriental rugs most commonly originate in Iran (Persia), Pakistan, Afghanistan, the Russian Caucasus, Turkey, China, and India. From these primary rug-producing countries are produced many varities.

RUG NOMENCLATURE

Carpets are referred to by the name of their place of origin, or by the name of the tribe which produced them. The following list includes the names of the most common carpets from the East, all of which are considered in this book.

Iran

Abadeh: town
Afshar: nomadic tribe
Ardebil: town
Bijar: town
Feraghan: province
Gorevan: village
Hamadan: town
Herat: town
Herez: town
Isfahan: town
Josheghan: town

Kashan: town
Khorassan: province
Kirman: town
Kurdistan: province
Luristan: district
Meshed: town
Qom: town
Sarouk: village
Senneh: town
Shiraz: town
Tabriz: town
Yzed: town

Caucasian

Cabistan: district
Chichi: tribe
Daghestan: province
Derbend: town

Karabagh: district
Kasak: tribe
Malgaran: tribe
Shirvan: district

Afghan: country	Bokhara: city and tribe *Turkoman*
Baluchi: tribe	Yomud: tribe

Bergama: town	Ladic: town *Turkish*
Ghiordes: town	Milas: town
Kula: district	Yuruk: tribe

Ning-Hsai: city	Tientsin: city *Chinese*
Samarkand: town	

All reproductions of rugs produced in Iran and other countries listed above.   *Pakistan & India*

Sarakhs Rug (note center medallion design page 52)

Motifs

One of the most interesting features of Oriental carpets is
the study of their designs. Thousands of forms are used,
some of which are common to many rug types, and others
more typical of specific rug-producing areas. It is difficult
to classify accurately all of the motifs, but some of the
more general design types are: geometric, floral, animal,
and medallion forms. Each of these design types has many
variations. It is fascinating to see how many ways a very
basic form is rendered. Some motifs are primitive in their
simplicity, yet a simple form may be embellished and
incorporated with other designs so that it becomes a mas-
terpiece in itself..

*types of
motifs*

*elegant
& simple*

Designs used in some rug-producing towns were so well
known that they were associated with only that town.

reproductions   Sarouk medallion designs and Tabriz hunting carpets are such examples. There are many reproductions of the most popular designs. Roumania currently produces hunting carpets in the style of the famous Tabriz rugs and India's rug industry is centered around Persian and Chinese reproductions. Additionally, within Iran and the Caucasus regions, there are improved roads, communications, and growing organization in the rug market. The majority of rugs produced are made for export, and as a result the motifs are becoming less and less a hallmark of a rug type.

Although it is extremely difficult to determine the origin of a carpet on the basis of its design, being able to identify the design features is helpful. There are certain types of carpets that incorporate general design characteristics and recognizing these features helps to narrow the list of possibilities.

general introduction   The following illustrations are an introduction to this fascinating study. By no means is this list complete, but it is representative of the various design forms, including geometric, floral and medallion styles used throughout the rug-producing districts.

Types of Motifs to follow:

Barber Pole Stripe
Butterfly
Candlestick
Caucasian Border
Chinese Fret
Chinese Wave
Cloud Band
Cock
Cross
Cypress
Dog
Endless Knot
Fish
Guli Hinnai
Herati Border
Jug & Comb

Latch Hook
Link
Lotus
Medallion
Mini Khani
Mir
Mirhab
Octagon
Palmette
Pole Medallion
Pomegranate
Rosette
Scorpion
Serrated Leaf
Snake
Star

Swastika
Tarantula
Triangle
Tree of Life

Trefoil
Turkoman Gul
Weeping Willow
Yin Yang
Zig Zag

Barber Pole Stripe

The pattern has some variations, but the stripes are always set at an angle and are invariably thin. The most common variation of this design is the use of small, secondary ornaments forming a pattern on each or every other stripe. The design is used extensively in Caucasian rugs.

Pakistan has recently begun production of many Caucasian rug styles and the barber pole stripe has, of course, been incorporated in these reproductions.

Butterfly

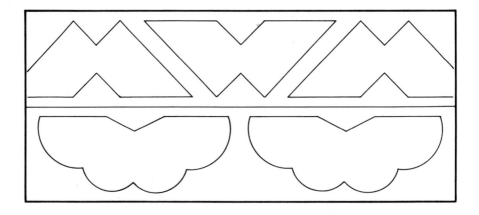

The butterfly motif is used mainly in Chinese and Caucasian rug design. The Caucasian style, typically geometric, most often appears in the borders. The Chinese rugs use this motif in the centerfield as well as in the borders. The style of the Chinese butterfly is realistic and highly ornamented, often with long flowing lines, and almost always the motif is sculptured.

All types of modern Chinese rugs have used various forms of the butterfly motif. The modern Caucasian rugs use the pattern rarely.

Candlestick

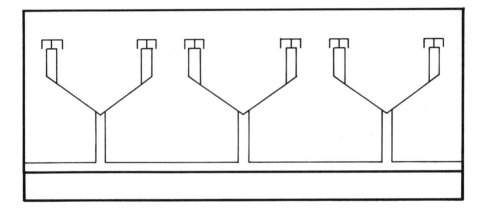

An ornament used in Turkoman rugs. The most frequent use of this motif is seen in small rugs used as door hangings. These are called Kachli rugs. The centerfield is divided into four sections, each displaying the motif. They are displayed either aligned or stacked, similar to either candlesticks or a candelabra.

The candlestick motif is typical of nomad rugs, almost exclusively to the Turkoman tribes.

Caucasian Border

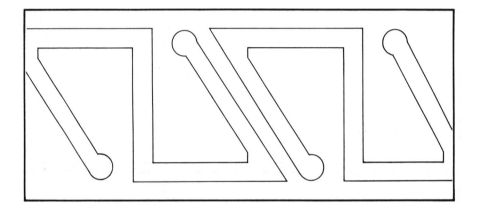

This design has been used in every type of Caucasian rug. The oldest known Caucasian examples display the motif only in the borders of the rugs, thus giving it its name. The modern pieces, however, often incorporate the pattern in the centerfield design in addition to its use in the borders. Some rugs produced in northeast Iran and some Pakistani reproductions have also incorporated the pattern.

Chinese Fret

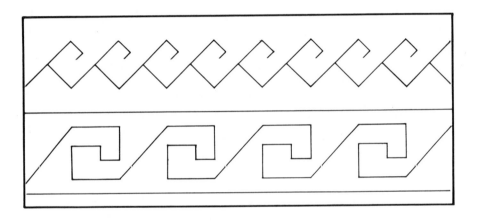

The design is alternatively called the Greek Key pattern. It is a typical motif in Chinese, Mongolian and Tibetan rugs. Some Caucasian weavers also use this as a border motif.

The pattern is used in Peking, Ning-Hsai, Tientsin and Kasak rugs. Currently, very few Indian and Pakistani reproductions incorporate the design.

Chinese Wave

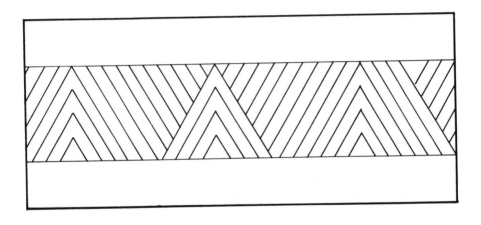

This is a design found in all forms of Chinese art. In rug-making, the wave pattern is used as a border motif. In older Chinese rugs, the wave appeared in the centerfield of rugs with landscape scenes, but these styles are not currently produced. The older Chinese rugs, with integrated centerfield scenes used this motif in conjunction with landscape designs. Today, the majority of Chinese rugs have stylized formats, medallion centerpieces and secondary ornamentation which includes the wave pattern.

Cloud Band

This motif was of Buddhist origin. First appearing in India it migrated to China and was used extensively in religious and non-religious art. The cloud band represents the heaven realms in Buddhist tradition. Persian weavers have also used the motif, and the proportions are quite similar to those of the Chinese cloud illustrated above, but the lines are rectangular instead of curved. The motif has no religious sigificance to the Persian weavers.

Cock

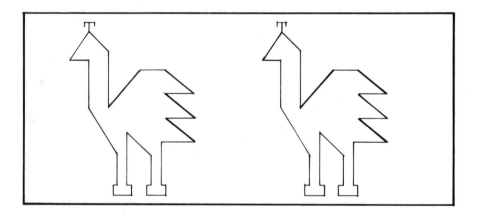

The cock is another animal motif used in Persian and Caucasian rugs. The nomads of Iran and the Russian Caucasus use this simple motif, and more elaborate renderings are used in Tabriz rugs.

It was a popular motif of the nomadic and semi-nomadic weavers who used their surroundings as a source of inspiration.

Cross

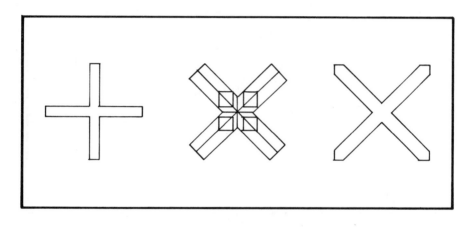

The cross as used in Oriental carpets has no religious significance. Iran is predominately Moslem, and the cross originates in folklore rather than in the religious heritage, as in Christian nations.

The cross takes varying forms throughout Iran and the Caucasus regions. It is rarely used in China.

Cypress

The motif appears in numerous types of Persian carpets. It is often elaborately ornamented, but the basic shape is consistent with the illustration above.

The cypress thrives in the more temperate regions of Iran, and it has been used by weavers as a symbol of eternal life. It is one of the few evergreens which thrives in Iran's often inclement weather, and in winter, the cypress may be the only greenery.

Dog

This motif appears in Tabriz hunting carpets and in nomadic Persian and Caucasian rugs. In the finest hunting carpets the motif is realistic, but the nomadic weavers incorporate a simple, somewhat primitive rendering as shown above.

The dog symbolizes companionship and protection to the nomadic weavers.

Endless Knot

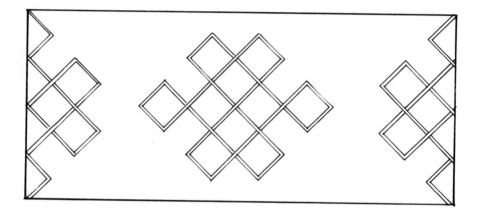

This popular design has been used in ceramic design, in fabrics, paintings and carvings for hundreds of Chinese temples. It has also been incorporated into rug design, and some of the modern Chinese rugs display the pattern in the borders. The endless Knot is one of the eight auspicious symbols of Buddhism.

Fish

The pattern is another of the eight auspicious symbols of Buddhism. It has been used in Chinese rugs and in some Tibetan and Mongolian ones; and recently some rugs originating from India have incorporated the pattern in the centerfields of Chinese reproductions.

Guli Hinnai

The motif is one which is used extensively in Persian rug production. It represents the flower of henna, a wildflower used as a dye source. The motif has a straight stem with usually three blossoms on either side.

The plant grows profusely throughout Iran, Turkey, etc. It is used for a textile dye and, in some cultures, as a hair and body coloring.

Herati Border

The name comes from the town of Herat, once belonging to Persia, and at one time a famous rug center. The Herat rugs met with such commercial success that the motif was eventually used in almost every rug type in Iran. The illustration above shows the original Herati pattern. Variations of the pattern are numerous, but all styles incorporate a central rosette flanked by serrated leaves.

Jug and Comb

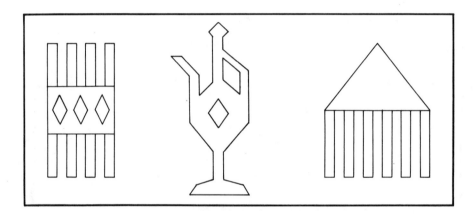

The jug and comb motifs frequently appear together. They are used on prayer rugs and on a few larger pieces. They symbolize purity and serve as a practical reminder for the devotee to wash and make the required preparations before prayer.

Turkish prayer rugs frequently incorporate the jug and comb motifs, but the pattern is also seen in Persian prayer rugs.

Latch Hook

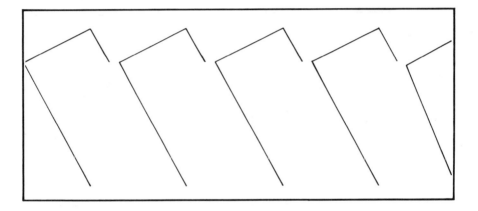

This motif is usually used as a border design. It is thought to be a variation of the swastika. Caucasian rugs frequently incorporate this motif in one or more border stripes.

Rugs typically using this motif include Kasak, Cabistan, Daghestan, Derbend, Chichi and some modern Pakistani reproductions of Caucasian designs.

Link Motif

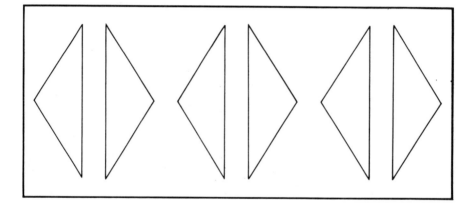

This motif is most typical of Caucasian rugs. It appears both in the borders and in the centerfield designs. Often coloring adds variation to the pattern. Sometimes three or four colors are alternated, adding interest to the simple pattern.

Look for this pattern in almost every type of Caucasian rug, and in the Pakistani reproductions of the designs of the Caucasus regions.

Lotus

The lotus is one of the eight auspicious symbols of Buddhism. It is used extensively in Chinese rugs. It is usually woven in white and a pale rose shade, invariably with some greenery surrounding it, or at its base. It is a symbol of purity and nobility.

The above illustrations show two forms of the lotus. The Chinese style is shown at the right. At the left is a form used in Iran. This style is sometimes confused with the pomegranate motif.

Medallion

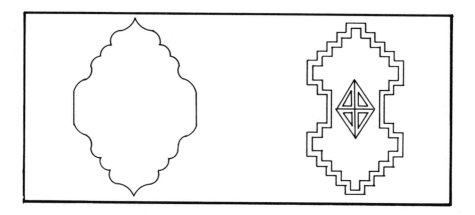

This motif has many forms and has been used in almost every variety of Persian, Caucasian and Chinese carpet. The medallion is used as a central single ornament, as seen in Kirman, Nain, and Tabriz carpets. It is also used in pairs, or in sets of three or more. The medallion in Caucasian rugs is always geometric, the Chinese is round, and Oersian carpets display varying forms of geometric, round, and floral medallions.

Mini Khani

Another very popular Persian floral motif is the Mini Khani. It is used in many rug types, but generally appears as an all-over, repeating pattern which forms a formal latticework in the centerfield. It always has a diamond-shaped center and five blossoms. The leaves may or may not appear.

Mir

This motif is known by various names, as the leaf, the Mir, The Mir-i-bota, the Seraband design, and the shawl pattern. It closely resembles the paisley which is said to represent the shape of the universe in Hindu literature. It is seen in many styles, ranging from a basic outlined shape to highly ornamented forms. It consistently has a top hook stape. Primarily the Mir is used in Persian and Indian rugs.

Mihrab

The mihrab is a feature of all prayer rugs. It is also called the prayer niche. Above are illustrations of some forms the mihrab takes. This is typical of rugs from Iran, Turkey, the Caucasus, and Afghanistan, and of other Turkoman pieces.

The above three illustrations are most typical of Turkish prayer rugs; however, since the mirhab styles vary considerably throughout the rug-making countries, it is difficult to classify them with total accuracy.

Octagon

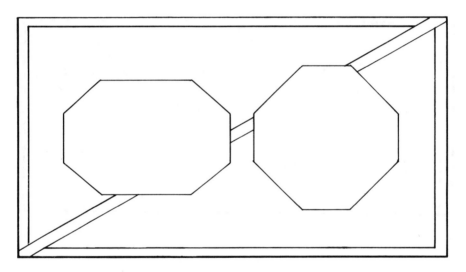

This form is prevalent in Turkoman rugs. It is frequently used as the primary motif, almost always as a repeating pattern covering the centerfield. The proportions vary somewhat. As a general rule, the octagon is as tall as it is wide in Afghan pieces. In Turkoman rugs, it is more frequently elongated, as seen in Yomud and Bokhara rugs. The arrangement of the form is aligned vertically and horizontally in some rugs, and aligned diagonally in others.

Palmette

The palmette motif is one of the most popular Persian rug decorations. It has been used primarily in floral styles, including Tabriz, Qom, Isfahan, and Kirman rugs, but it does also appear in some rugs with more geometric stylizing.

Pole Medallion

The design is most frequently used in Hamadan rugs. It is sometimes rendered with rectangular ends as is shown above, or with floral extensions. It is used as a centerfield motif.

Some Turkish rugs, usually small, and some camel bags have used variations of the pole medallion as centerfield designs.

Pomegranate

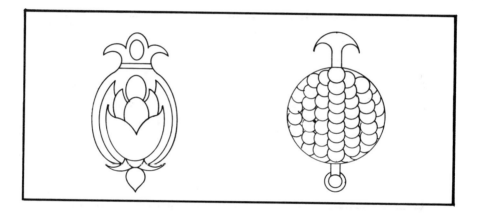

The motif is typical of Persian floral carpets. Some forms resemble renderings of Egyptian origin, very formal and highly stylized, and others are more natural and flowing. The pomegranate symbolizes fertility.

The pomegranate has been used in Tabriz, Qom, and in Roumanian carpets.

Rosette

Of all the floral patterns used in Persian rugs, the rose is by far the most popular. It has been used in every Persian rug type, from very simple nomad renderings, to the most elaborate carpets made in Sarouk, Isfahan and Tabriz.

Elaborate floral gardens were kept as part of the royal palaces in Shiraz, and the early carpets from this area, including most of those from the Fergahan district, were resplendent with variations of the rosette pattern.

Scorpion

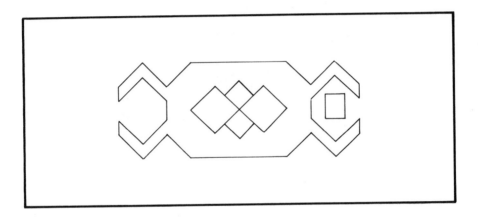

The scorpion is usually geometric in shape. The scorpion symbol is seen in most types of Caucasian works and some nomadic Turkoman rugs. The scorpion is native to Iran and the surrounding areas. Some species are extremely poisonous, yet most are not deadly, but with little protection from the elements, the nomadic weavers were constantly aware of imminent danger. The scorpion pattern was possibly used as a type of talisman to ward off attacks.

Serrated Leaf

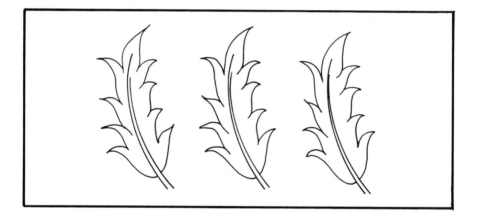

This design is used extensively throughout Iran. It is most frequently used with floral ornaments in both the centerfield and the borders. The serrated leaf is also incorporated as part of the Mini Khani and Herati motifs.

Many older carpets from Fergahan, Shiraz and Kirman represented the serrated leaf pattern. Modern Qom and Tabriz rugs also use the design extensively.

Snake

This motif is alternately termed the 'S' design. It usually appears very stylized, as in Caucasian pieces.

The snake symbolizes wisdom. Two snake forms are represented above. Both forms are used in Caucasian rugs, but the Persian preference is for the curved style. The Chinese snake form is quite different, usually it is represented as a circular pattern, a snake biting its tail. The Chinese use this motif to represent eternity.

Star

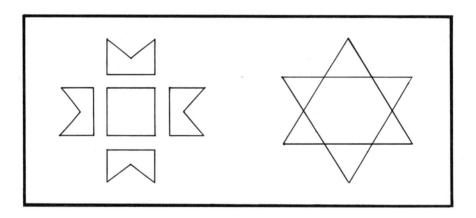

Basically two forms are used, the six-pointed and the eight-pointed star. The six-pointed star was adapted from the Star of David, and evolved as a good luck talisman to the Moslem people. The eight-pointed star represents the jewel of Mohammed. These star motifs are typical of Turkoman and Caucasian rugs.

Swastika

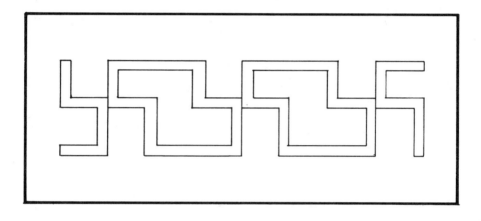

This symbol has been used by a variety of cultures, and is one of the oldest known to man. Cave paintings, Egyptian pottery, Greek and Chinese art provide abundant examples of its early use.

The swastika's use in carpet design has been most prominent in Chinese and Caucasian products. It is the symbol of good luck and prosperity.

Tarantula

This motif is used primarily in Turkoman rugs. It is rendered in various forms, but is always geometric in shape.

The bite of the tarantula is poisonous, and though seldom fatal, it is extremely painful. The motif is woven as a form of symbolic protection.

Triangle

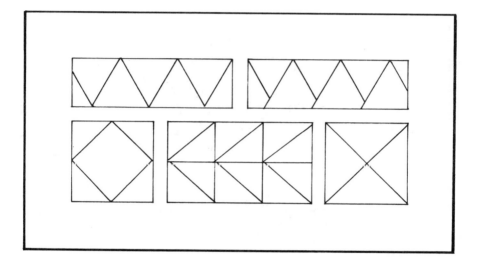

This basic form is incorporated in all types of Caucasian rugs, in some Persian and Turkish rugs, but seldom in Turkoman pieces. It is combined in various ways, often with coloring to give the optical illusion of figure ground reversal. It is an earth symbol connoting stability and balance.

Five of the most common triangle patterns are illustrated above.

Tree of Life

The Tree of Life motif is one which is used in almost every type of Persian, Turkish and Caucasian rug. It is frequently used as a large centerfield design and has two basic forms. The pattern is realistically produced in Tabriz, Isfahan and Qom rugs, but the nomadic weavers, including those of the Caucasus region, use a geometric form.

Trefoil

This pattern is used as a repeating motif, generally in border stripes, also called the reciprocal trefoil. It is frequently seen in Caucasian work and some Persian Seraband carpets.

The pattern's origin is unknown, but, like the swastika, is is used in many varying cultures with distinct historical and religious heritages.

Turkoman Gul

This variation of the octagon pattern is used solely in Turkoman rugs. It is always elongated as shown, approximately two thirds as high as it is wide in Bokhara rugs; the Afghan Gul, however, is almost always square in shape. The pattern is used as an all-over, repeating design in the centerfield of Turkoman rugs.

Weeping Willow

This motif is common to some Persian rugs, especially the cemetery carpets. These rugs were woven by a family, with each member making a contribution. The carpet was later spread on the grave of the deceased.

This motif also appeared in some of the older Chinese pieces, distinguished by an odd number of branches, three, five or seven.

Yin Yang

The symbol is used in Chinese rugs as a central medallion and in the borders. One side is dark, the other light. It symbolizes the unity of existence in opposites.

The design has become one of the best known of Chinese origin. The Yin Yang, along with most other Chinese motifs, evolved along with the religious philosophies that have dominated Chinese history.

Zig Zag

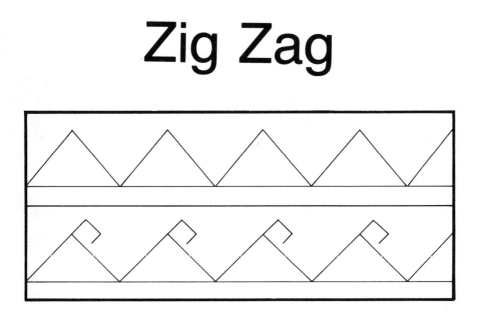

The motif is used primarily as a secondary motif, as a border ornament, and to accent other designs. The zig zag design is used primarily as a border ornament in Persian and Caucasian rugs. It is also used as an embellishment to a prominent central motif, such as for medallions. It symbolizes eternity in the form of running water.

The zig zag pattern is frequently confused with the Chinese fret or the latch hook motif.

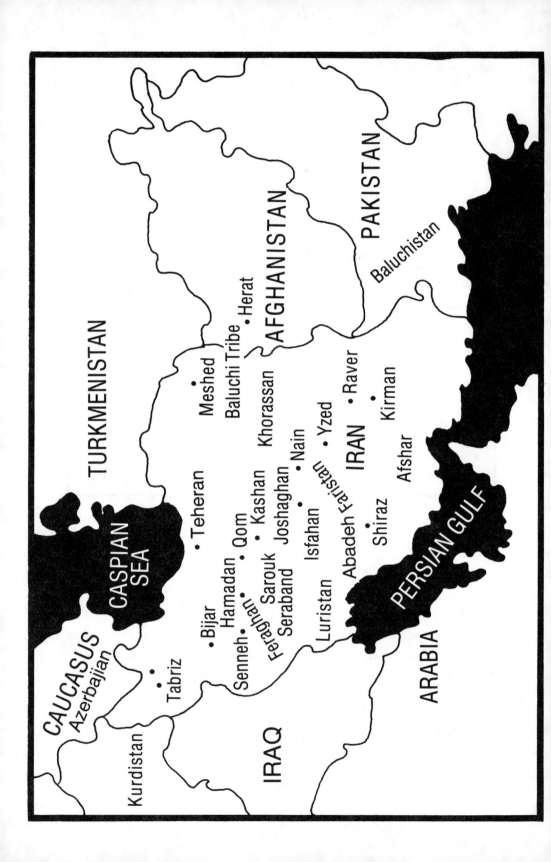

Persian Rugs

Persian rugs are products of Iran, which was known as Persia until 1935. The rugs are handmade in factories employing upwards of fifteen weavers, and by individuals, families, and small groups as a cottage industry.

rug making

The rugs produced in factories tend to be standardized in respect to materials, dyes, knotting, and patterns. The weavers are employed to produce specific products and to follow directions supplied by their employers. As a result there are few variations in factory-made rugs. There are also a limited number of special order rugs produced for individuals and export firms. Qom and Nain are two of the most prominent sources of factory rugs, and they produce some of the finest in Iran today.

factory rugs

*rug
export*

Nomadic weavers and village craftsmen produce approximately 70 percent of the rugs in Iran. The majority of these rugs are exported, and currently the Western countries provide the largest market for them. The leading countries of purchase are the United States, Germany, England and Switzerland.

*Jufi
knots*

Identifying Persian rugs can be difficult. There are many variations in design, technique of weave, wool, dyes and sizes. The designs are diverse, but if a general type were to be named, the floral patterns are most typical of Persian rugs. The techniques of weave are also diverse. The two basic knot forms are used, Persian and Turkish, as well as the Jufi knot in poor quality pieces. The side and end finishes incorporate overcast and selvaged sides, and fringed and selvaged ends. The wool grades range from soft, shiny wool of the Kirman rugs to the coarser, somewhat dull wool seen in Hamadan rugs. Dyes currently used are almost all synthetic. There are, however, some nomadic Persian rugs still dyed with natural substances, but these are the exception. Regarding rug sizes, the Persian rugs are made in all ranges, though not all types are produced in large, room-sized carpets.

The chapters in this section provide an outline on some of the better known Persian rug types. The brief sketches provide information for the interested buyer and for those just interested in learning about this fascinating art-form.

Types of Persian Rugs to Follow:

Abadeh	Kashan
Afshar	Khorassan
Ardebil	Kirman
Bijar	Kurdistan
Feraghan	Luristan
Gorevan	Meshed
Hamadan	Qom
Herat	Sarouk
Herez	Senneh
Isfahan	Shiraz
Josheghan	Tabriz
	Yzed

Boy Weavers of Tabriz (circ. 1900)

Abadeh

Abadeh is a city approximately 100 miles north of Shiraz. Carpets have been produced there only within the past fifty years. The weavers are excellent craftsmen, and produce extremely durable rugs. The most popular design currently woven has been adapted from the Kashkai tribal pattern. The two rugs are distinguishable in that the tribal products are more intricately rendered and the colors deeper than in the Abadeh rugs.

pattern similarities

Since rug production was organized in this city relatively recently, there are no antiques. The earliest Abadeh carpets were of a design which was not commercially successful in the East. Those carpets had all-over patterns of formal vases with red, orange, and blue-gray flowers. The centerfield color was generally of a cream tone. These carpets were exported to the western countries where the demand was greatest.

vase patterns

The most common Abadeh carpet in production today is somewhat geometric in design. It incorporates a pointed, centered medallion with corner ornamentation. The main border and sometimes the centerfield are decorated with colorful floral motifs, and various geometric forms. The floral vase pattern mentioned above is still produced, but this style is not nearly as common.

geometric styles

medallion
centerfield

Centered medallion on a yellow, red, or blue field is the most common pattern. The carpet often has numerous small ornaments decorating the field, and the primary border is covered with geometric flowers on a white or yellow background.

colors

The background color in Abadeh carpets is usually red, dark blue or mustard yellow. The secondary colors are numerous, usually including shades of blue, ivory, white, yellow, red, green and brown. The carpets are bright and very colorful.

quick
reference

1. Warp and Woof: Cotton.

2. Pile: Tightly knotted, medium length, very durable.

3. Knots: Persian.

4. Sides: Overcast with colored yarn.

5. Ends: Fringed white warp threads.

6. Sizes: Usually around seven feet or less.

7. Colors: Red, blue, gold, ivory, green, mustard, earth tones.

Afshar

Afshar is a Persian nomadic tribe after which these carpets were named. There are actually two tribes producing rugs, one is marketed as Afshar and the other as Kirman-Afshar. There are differences between these two rug types. The former is quite heavy and somewhat coarse; the latter is more akin to the soft carpets of the Kirman region.

two types

The antique Afshar rugs were commonly woven on a wool foundation using Turkish knots. They were heavy and durable carpets. Frequently the ends were finished with braided, looped fringe and the sides were overcast in multiple colors of wool yarn. There were usually three or more borders surrounding the centerfield, one being wide with the narrower borders on either side. The primary colors were dark red, green, yellow, blue, pink, and earth tones. Frequently in weaving, these colors were made to appear shaded by the use of subtle variations in tone. Designs of the antique rugs were somewhat irregular and scattered throughout the centerfield. Floral patterns and occasionally the Herati pattern were used, but no one design was typical of this rug type.

braided fringe

color shading

The Afshar carpets available today are mostly of the Kirman-Afshar variety. These rugs are very soft and pliable. They are made of a fine, lustrous wool which is similar to the wool in Kirman rugs. These carpets are

soft wools

woven on a cotton foundation with more attention to detail than the antiques. The colors are usually dark shades of blue and brown, with highlights of red and ivory. Although there are modern Afshar rugs woven that are quite light in overall appearance, the color blends are never highly contrasting. The carpets are not large, most commonly ranging up to eight feet in length.

blending tones

The modern Afshars, for the most part, are medallion-style rugs. Sometimes there are two centered medallions enclosed in a hexagon-shaped field. On these rugs there are also small motifs covering the centerfield and corners. Another popular design is the Mir-i-botah. Occasionally a stylized tree of life appears as part of the centerfield design.

Most commonly the colors in Afshar rugs tend to be dark, usually shades of blue and brown. Touches of lighter and brighter colors accent the carpets. Red and ivory are common, and yellow and sometimes blue are also used.

quick reference

1. Warp and Woof: Cotton in the modern rugs.

2. Pile: Medium in length.

3. Knots: Turkish.

4. Sides: Overcast, sometimes in more than one color.

5. Ends: Fringed.

Ardebil

Ardebil is a town in the Province of Azerbaijan on the western shore of the Caspian Sea. The town is known for the famous carpet discovered in one of its mosques. This carpet, incidentally, was not produced in the town, but in Kashan, and is now part of the permanent collection on display at the Victoria and Albert Museum, London.

museum piece

Rug making has continued uninterrupted for the past few hundred years, and the designs have remained somewhat simple. Basic rounded medallions with floral ornamentation appearing on a plain centerfield form the most common pattern. These rugs will often have corner motifs and three to five decorated border stripes.

antique rugs

simple designs

The modern Ardebil carpets have changed dramatically from those produced up to forty years ago. The rugs now produced reflect a distinctive Caucasian flavor in design and workmanship. Primarily the carpets available today incorporate geometric motifs similar to those of Kasak carpets. The colors, however, are usually more varied. These rugs are also available in larger sizes than were the antiques, ranging up to approximately nine feet in length.

geometric forms

The geometric, Caucasian-type designs are the most common patterns. Rare antiques incorporated some of the more carefully executed patterns, but these are no longer produced. Typically, the carpets have a medallion center with border ornamentation. The centerfield will display secondary designs, but these are never used as an all-over repeating pattern.

colors

These vary widely, but usually the colors incorporated in one piece are limited to three or four shades. Combinations of red, blue, green, beige, peach, yellow or brown are most typical in the modern rugs.

quick reference

1. Warp and Woof: Cotton.

2. Pile: Loosely woven, medium length.

3. Knots: Turkish.

4. Sides: Overcast, often in bright colored wool.

5. Ends: Fringed, sometimes quite long.

6. Sizes: Not over nine feet in length.

7. Colors: Blue, red, beige, yellow, peach and green.

Bijar

Bijar is a town located in Western Iran in the province of Kurdistan. It is approximately 30 miles northeast of Senneh. Being so close to this famous rug center, it is understandable that there are some similarities in their textile products.

kurdistan product

Bijar carpets are distinctive for their heaviness. The foundation threads as well as the yarn used to form the pile are thick. Because of this feature there are fewer knots per square inch, and the resulting designs are not as refined as the neighboring Senneh products. Stylized floral motifs, birds, animals and human figures were typical motifs in the older rugs.

heaviness, a feature

The modern products from Bijar and outerlying regions are produced in a wide range of patterns and color combinations. Patterns typical of Kirman, Senneh and Sarouk are produced, but the Bijar products are nonetheless distinguishable by their heaviness. In comparison to other Persian rugs, the Bijar rugs are the heaviest made.

Probably the most typical style produced today is a carpet with a centered medallion and elaborate corner pieces. Inscriptions have also been a common feature. But as the carpets are primarily produced for export, styles that are the most marketable are the ones produced. Over the

many designs

years, tastes of the buying public have changed, and this has been reflected in the great variety of motifs used in the Bijar rugs.

color   The field of modern Bijar carpets is often a camel color, similar to that in many Hamadan carpets. Others incorporate red, blue, green, yellow, white and ivory as background tones and for ornamentation highlights.

quick reference

1. Warp and Woof: Wool and cotton, extremely heavy.

2. Pile: Stiff, heavy and somewhat long.

3. Knots: Turkish.

4. Sides: Overcast.

5. Ends: Selvaged, sometimes a fringe woven on. The web of one end is sometimes turned back and hemmed.

6. Sizes: Medium, up to about 9 x 12 feet.

7. Colors: Camel, red, blue, green, white, ivory and yellow.

Feraghan

The plain of Feraghan, which is seven thousand feet above sea level and surrounded by mountains, lies just west of the line of travel between Teheran and Isfahan. The mountains of this region resemble the Highlands of Scotland. The hillsides support pasturage for sheep and are carpeted with flowers, including tulips, irises, narcissi, carnations, red anemonies, scarlet poppies, yellow snapdragons, and henna blossoms.

floral abundance

Feraghan carpets have basically two characteristic designs. One of the designs is the Herati pattern, with its flowers enclosed in stylized cloud motifs. The other pattern is the Flower of Henna, with tree shapes of yellow flowers arranged in rows throughout the centerfield, these are usually surrounded by a profusion of floral motifs. Occasionally, thise rugs have a medallion center, comprising a tulip and other flowers set in the center of a floral field. Sometimes a rug is seen with flower stalks in the center with gracefully curved vine and floral ornamentation surrounding the stalks. Whatever the design though, the garlands of flowers are an essential element in the design and are usually rendered in subdued tones. Borders are an important feature of these carpets, the ground of the widest is often of a soft green, and includes wavy lines that connect floral patterns.

flower of Henna

numerous borders

*longer
pile*

Modern Feraghan carpets have retained the traditional designs and colors of the antiques, but the overall tone appears much brighter and the designs are less carefully executed. The pile is also longer than that of the finest antiques, and the texture is visibly coarse. Knots used in the modern carpets are Turkish and less tightly woven than the Persian knots of the older carpets.

color

The antique rugs are more somber in tone than the modern products. The dyes were from natural sources and red or blue usually predominated. Highlights of green, yellow, ivory and blue were typical combinations. The modern pieces are more varied, but still red and blue are the most popular colors.

*quick
reference*

1. Warp and Woof: Cotton, sometimes woof dyed blue or red.

2. Pile: Usually long, evenly clipped and somewhat coarse.

3. Knots: Persian in antique, Turkish in modern.

4. Sides: Overcast, sometimes with black wool.

5. Ends: Fringed white warp threads.

6. Sizes: Small to large, room-sized carpets.

7. Colors: Subdued in antiques, brighter in modern.

Gorevan

Gorevan rugs are manufactured in the northwestern area of Iran in the Azerbaijan district. This is the same district in which Tabriz, Herez and Meshed carpets are produced. The weavers, however, have never rivaled the refined textiles of their neighboring Tabriz weavers. They have continued to use somewhat corsely spun wool and incorporated this into carpets with a distinctive primitive feel.

coarse wool

Antique Gorevan rugs are not collectors' pieces. There are few exceptional antiques. The majority of these rugs are loosely knotted, coarse-looking rugs. The wool used in their manufacture and the designs rendered gave them a somewhat crude appearance. Usually the designs in Gorevan rugs are not particularly detailed. There will invariably be two or more concentric medallions centered on the carpet, with these medallions sometimes repeated over the entire centerfield. Embellishments are added to the centerfield and to the medallion: these are usually leaves and large figures. There is, generally, one main border stripe, often with two or three minor stripes to either side. These borders are usually ornamented with the turtle pattern.

medallion patterns

Modern Gorevan rugs are usually found in larger sizes, and more likely than not, square in shape. Still, as in the antiques, the designs are crude, neither highly refined nor

square shapes

*turtle
border*

elaborately embellished. Centered medallions are common, as is the turtle border design. Often the carpets have been washed to bring out some luster in the coarse wools. The colors most frequently incorporated in these carpets are lighter shades, though the borders may be primarily woven of dark blue or red.

Concentric medallions, with rectangular lines, the medallions are often covered with crude motifs of leaves, vines and sometimes flowers. The designs are usually positioned symmetrically, and are repetitious. Turtle designs are common in the borders.

colors

Tan, red, dark blue, white, green and yellow are the predominant colors in these carpets. Generally they have a light appearance, and are predominated by dark colors only in the borders.

*quick
reference*

1. Warp and Woof: Cotton sometimes the weft threads are dyed blue or red.

2. Pile: Medium in length, of somewhat coarse wool.

3. Knots: Turkish, quite loosely woven.

4. Sides: Selvaged.

5. Ends: Fringe.

6. Sizes: Large, carpet sizes, usually ten feet and up.

Hamadan

Hamadan is located in the northwestern part of Iran. The ancient city of Hamadan predates the Christian era and has been the principal marketplace for wares produced in the city and surrounding villages for centuries. Wool is an important product of the district, which is processed, dyed, and woven locally. The majority of rugs marketed as Hamadan pieces are produced in the villages surrounding the city itself.

ancient city

The use of natural camel hair was a typical feature of early Hamadan rugs. Usually it was incorporated in the centerfield and as the background in the main border stripe. Under magnification, camel hair appears very smooth, with no fibrous extentions, as does wool yarn. Herati patterns, the pole medallion and floral designs were common ornamentation. Yellow, blue, red brown were the typical colors. Hamadan rugs were woven with Turkish knots.

camel hair

Hamadan rugs are plentiful, and are available in a wide variety of designs, color combinations and sizes. Camel hair is still used, but tan wool is becoming a common substitute. However, almost all rugs of this type still have a camel-color background in the centerfield and in the main border. Their texture is somewhat rough, and the wool has a dull appearance. They are durable rugs, and are still

rough texture

Turkish knots

woven with the Turkish knot exclusively. A feature typical of these rugs is the use of two or more weft threads between each row of knots. Viewing the carpet from the back, an uneven pattern appears, giving it a very textured appearance.

colors

Hamadan rugs invariably have a predominance of tan hues. Originally this was achieved by the use of undyed camel hair, but today wool is used. Other colors include green, red, blue, yellow and ivory.

quick reference

1. Warp and Woof: Cotton in modern carpets, wool and sometimes camel hair in antique carpets.

2. Pile: Firm, but not densely knotted, medium length.

3. Knots: Turkish, frequently with extra warp threads between knotted rows.

4. Sides: Overcast.

5. Ends: Fringed.

6. Colors: Camel, green, blue, red, yellow, brown and ivory.

Herat

Just across the border of Iran in Afghanistan, is the old Persian city of Herat. Situated approximately 100 miles from the current Iranian border, Herat is in the direct line of travel between Bokhara and Cashmere, as well as between Meshed and the East. Historically Herat was the marketplace for the products of the Khorassan district as well as all surrounding villages. There were four large bazaars all located under one dome which served as the commercial center.

marketplace

These carpets were some of the most skillfully woven, incorporating many intricate patterns including the palmette, traceries, and of course, the Herati pattern. Some of the earlier rugs were woven on a silk foundation. The designs of the Herat carpets are very similar to some from Feraghan. The Herati pattern was generally used as an all-over motif, and the distinguishing feature was that the motif was small and more ornate than in other rugs. The colors of these carpets usually tended to dark tones of blue or red. The center border was usually green, ivory, yellow, red and blue. These rugs were tightly woven and very closely cropped.

antique rugs

palm design

The carpets produced in and around the city of Herat are dramatically different. They are of the Turkoman style; refer to the Turkoman section for information on the modern pieces.

modern rugs

Herati
pattern

The Herati pattern was the trademark of these carpets. The motif became very popular and was eventually used in rug design throughout Iran. The turtle design and various forms of the pear, palmette and floral motifs were also used.

colors

The overall tone of the Herat carpets was usually somber, with dark blue and red predominating. Frequently gold, yellow and mustard shades highlighted intricate motifs. Secondary colors included green, lighter shades of blue, brown and orange.

quick
reference

1. Warp and Woof: Wool, cotton and rarely silk.

2. Pile: Closely cropped, others of medium length pile.

3. Knots: Always Turkish.

4. Sides: Overcast.

5. Ends: Narrow web of fringe with loose warp threads at each end.

6. Sizes: Usually up to seven feet, some runners and saddlebags.

7. Colors: Red, green, blue, yellow, ivory.

Herez

Herez is located in the mountain district of Azerbaijan, east of Tabriz and southwest of the Caspian Sea. The terrain is rugged and the people are primarily nomadic and semi-nomadic. Herez carpets originally included the products of the surrounding villages as well as some carpets produced in Tabriz and Sultanbad.

The oldest examples of Herez rugs are not particularly outstanding. The quality improved somewhat around the turn of this century. The antique carpets were similar in texture to those of Hamadan, rough texture with approximately the same number of knots per square inch. The designs were large and pronounced, with center medallions in blue or ivory, on open fields of light or dark red, light blue, brown, or tan. They are characteristically brilliant, and were frequently used in the lobbies of hotels.

Today, Herez rugs are still produced, but they seem to be more readily available in Germany and Switzerland, than in other Western countries. The rugs, marketed as Herez today include Gorevan, Serapi and Bakshaish carpets. The quality of some is excellent, with fine detail, and densely knotted fine wool. The Serapi and Bakshaish are the finest examples of this type. They feature more refined colors than the Gorevan pieces, and have somewhat shorter piles.

*stylized
motifs*

Geometric plant designs, central medallions with some ornamentation on an open field. Borders often incorporate the palm design, vases and lotus blossoms.

colors

Red and off-white are probably the most popular and predominate colors in the modern rugs. Blue yellow, green and brown tones are also intermingled, but these usually are secondary colors.

*quick
reference*

1. Warp and Woof: Cotton.

2. Pile: Varied, better rugs have shorter nap.

3. Knots: Turkish.

4. Sides: Overcast.

5. Ends: Short fringe.

6. Sizes: Large, room-sized rugs, many up to 16 feet in length, many almost square.

7. Colors: Finer rugs have more subdued colors. Red, blue, brown, and sometimes camel are the most common.

Color section commentary:

Page 1 - Bokhara rug. Close up of border. Note variation of Turkoman Gul in border (see page 70). More of this rug on page 3.

Page 2 - Shirvan Khilim. A classical example of a khilim rug (see page 12 for description). This one is carefully woven, firm and durable.

page 3 - Bokhara rug on page one only this time we see the centerfield. Note how well the medallions fit description on page 178.

Page 4 & 5 - Classical example of Abadeh rug (see page 79),. Close up on page 4 shows how intricate the floral designs really are. Also note crosses and zig zags (both very common to Persian rugs).

Page 6 - Kazak rug. Note zig zag border and how hatch hook is incorporated into central medallions. Note how central field fits description on page 144.

Page 7 - Bergama Prayer rug. Excellent example of Turkish Prayer Rug (see page 55). One faces the rug to Mecca and prostrates touching their forehead to the crown of the Mirhab. This rug can be used by 3 family members together. Note also the typical Bergama side border (see page 158).

Page 8 - Hamadan rug. Note predominance of Tan color (see page 92). Note also that the color, even from the same vat of dye, can vary greatly because vats are not highly controlled (see page 132). Here the blue is sometimes very bright and sometimes almost black. Many buyers fail to look for this in shopping.

Front cover - same as page 4.

Back Cover - Antique Chinese Cushion Rug. At 48 Senneh knots to the square inch, it is not considered tightly woven. It does, however, have excellent fluffy wool pile and one can not expect to have both (a choice the buyer is wise to reflect on).

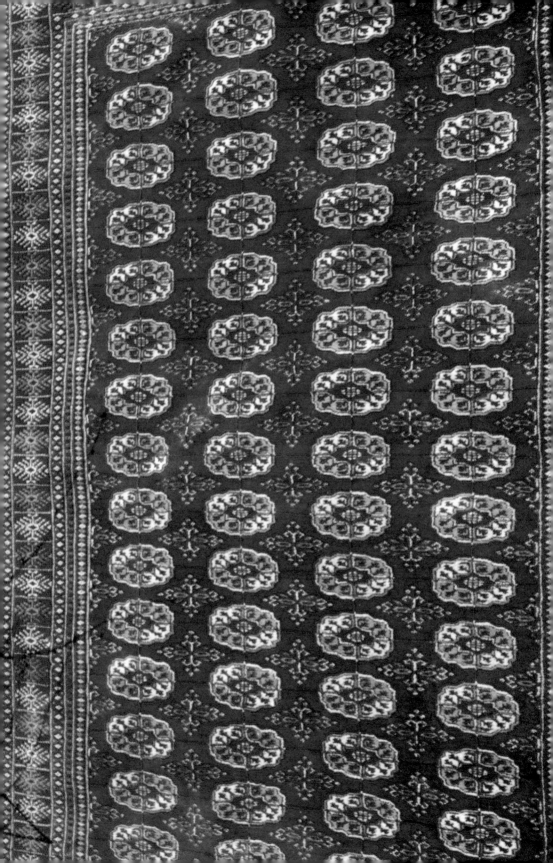

uneven   appears on the back of the rug. This irregularity is a result of uneven weft threads: some are spun thicker than others, and appear nubbly in texture.

intricate
designs   The modern Isfahan products are primarily ornamented with a centered, round medallion and with palmette and floral designs connected by vines. The designs are very intricate, similar in fashion to the neighboring carpet district, where Nain rugs are manufactured.

color   The color range used in the Isfahan rugs is very rich, and varied. These are some of the more colorful carpets produced in Iran. The most commonly used colors are dark red, indigo, gold, yellow and green. The centerfield is usually red or dark blue with white.

quick
reference   1. Warp and Woof: Cotton.

2. Pile: Short, quality wool.

3. Knots: Both Persian and Turkish.

4. Ends: Web with loose warp threads.

5. Sizes: Usually under six feet in length.

6. Colors: Red, indigo, yellow, green, gold and white.

Isfhahan

Isfahan is a city located in the commercial center of Iran. The production of carpets was at its height in the sixteenth and seventeenth centuries, when Isfahan was the capital city of Persia. With the invasion of the Afghan hordes, rug production was disrupted until the early twentieth century.

Antique Isfahan carpets are of the finest quality and are extremely rare. These carpets were woven in wool and silk, the more elaborate examples had silver and gold threads ornamenting the centerfield designs. The motifs of the antique rugs were intricately woven on a background of crimson or deep wine red. These included large palmettes or rich floral patterns, proportionately distributed and connected by vines. The rugs displayed one wide border between two narrow ones, often with palmettes between serrated leaves on a yellow field. The carpets were very thin and tightly knotted. Both the Persian and the Turkish knot forms were used.

Modern Isfahan carpets have been produced only since the early twentieth century, following the end of World War I. These carpets are becoming more plentiful and are still of excellent quality. The rugmakers have continued to incorporate the traditional designs. A feature of the modern Isfahan carpets is the irregular pattern which

Josheghan

Josheghan is a small town north of Isfahan and south of Kashan, located near the northeast rim of the Zagros Mountain Range. The terrain surrounding the outer areas of the town is composed of regions with severe climatic conditions, with an annual rainfall usually less than twenty inches. But the town's immediate surrounding lands, where fertile fields, orchards, and palm groves have flourished for centuries, are in dramatic contrast to these desert-like conditions.

fertile fields

Antique Josheghan carpets made in the 1700s and in the first part of the 1800s were the finest of their products. The patterns differ significantly from the modern carpets of today. The finest examples preserved reveal the elaborate renderings of floral patterns displayed in the centerfield of the carpets. Elongated palms, rosettes and peonies were common motifs.These were often enclosed in a framework of interconnecting diamond shapes that adorned the entire field of the carpet. The borders, usually one main surrounded on each side by one very narrow accent border, were woven in a contrasting shade to that of the centerfield. These borders incorporated smaller flowers and diamond motifs, similar to those appearing as the primary design.

floral pattern

The modern carpets vary in quality. There seem to be two

*varying
qualities*

standards of weave manufactured, and onesells for approximately 30 percent more than the other. The higher priced carpets are tighter in weave and as a result, the design resolution is finer. However, the Josheghan carpets with fewer knots per square inch have a softer appearance, with the motifs less distinct. The modern rugs are available in large room-sized varieties as well as smaller area rugs.

*design
features*

Generally, a type of scroll carried throughout the margin of the field, and forming medallions, is popular. Another common design is a series of crosses with angular ends and adorned with floral figures; also, the eight-pointed star is used in conjunction with the croes. There are frequently many four and six-petalled roses.

*quick
reference*

1. Warp and Woof: Cotton.

2. Pile: Fine wool of medium length.

3. Knots: Turkish.

4. Sides: Overcast.

5. Ends: A thin narrow web and fringe.

6. Sizes: Area rug sizes up to sixteen feet in length.

Kashan

Kashan is a city located south of Qom and northeast of Isfahan and serviced by a railway running north from Kirman to Teheran. The town's population is under 100,000. Historically, Kashan was the center of the silk rug industry in Persia.

The famous Ardebil carpet, now displayed in the Victoria and Albert Museum, London, was made in Kashan. It is one of the most famous carpets in existence. This carpet is exceptional for its size, over thirty-four feet long by seventeen feet wide, and for its suprb craftsmanship.

Ardebil carpet

Today, some of the finest Persian carpets are still manufactured in Kashan and in its surrounding villages. Silk carpets continue to be produced, and these are of extremely fine quality. The silk carpets are usually woven entirely of silk (on a silk warp and woof). The woolen Kashan carpets are woven on a cotton foundation, with Persian knots, usually quite firm and with medium to short pile. There are also some carpets made in a combination of silk and wool.

silk rugs

The most common motif of the Kashan carpet is a medallion centered on a field of interconnected floral designs. The corner ornamentation mirrors the central medallion.

design   Also some floral vase patterns are produced. One feature
                  of the Kashan carpets is the ornamented centerfield.

color   Dark blue, red, and green, also rose, turquoise, deep wine
                  red and ivory are the most common colors used today. The
                  overall appearance is subdued and soft.

quick   1. Warp and Woof: Cotton or silk.
reference
                  2. Pile: Modern carpets have medium length pile, the
                  older carpets were clipped shorter.

                  3. Knots: Persian.

                  4. Sides: Overcast with wool or silk.

                  5. Ends: Short web with loose warp threads at each end.

                  6. Sizes: Up to 9 x 12.

                  7. Colors: Blue, red, green, rose, turquoise, wine red and
                  ivory.

Khorassan

Khorassan is located in northeastern Iran, a province separated from Russia to the north by mountains, and from Afghanistan to the east by a salt desert. The terrain is varied, including alpine tracts, irrigated fields, and desert regions. The inhabitants of Khorassan include a variety of ethnic groups, and various nomadic tribes. Meshed is the largest city of the province and is the main distribution point for carpets produced in the Khorassan province.

Khorassan rugs are among the finest antiques, but are very scarce. One feature of some of the finer rugs is the sculpturing of the pile so the figures appear to stand out from the background. There are frequently numerous borders surrounding the centerfield, occasionally as many as ten or twelve. The centerfield motifs included the palm pattern at each corner which extended to form a rosette in the center. Others had the palm and rosette covering the entire field. The diamond Herati pattern was not used until the early 1900s, so it will not appear on Khorassan rugs prior to that date.

These rugs have retained the use of many ornamental borders, usually one being wide with many narrow ones on either side. Floral patterns, connecting wavy lines, rosettes and the palm are border decorations common to the modern rugs. The central designs are more varied than

varied pattern

in the older rugs, and these include the use of the Herati pattern, lions, gazelles, and various types of birds. An elongated palm pattern is also typical, usually red on a blue background. Another pattern incorporated is the central medallion, and sometimes two medallions on a plain background. Floral Khorassan rugs often have symmetrical arrangements, but not as flowing or delicate as some other Persian floral carpets. There are also some carpets with ornamented stripes known as the Barber Pole design, and in most instances, these have small Herati patterns woven into the stripes.

quick reference

1. Warp and Woof: Cotton, sometimes the woof threads are dyed blue or red.

2. Pile: Usually long, evenly clipped.

3. Knots: Persian in the antiques, Turkish in modern rugs.

4. Sides: Overcast, sometimes with black wool.

5. Ends: Fringed white warp threads.

6. Sizes: Small to large room-sized carpets.

7. Colors: Subdued in antiques, brighter in modern carpets, dark blue field, sometimes with soft red and ivory, yellow, green, and red.

Kirman

Kirman is an old Persian district and a city located between the Desert of Lut and the Arabian Sea. It is the most southeasterly commercial center. As Kirman was located outside of the major trade routes, rug production was not readily influenced by outsiders. The inhabitants are scattered, but the city population is rapidly growing. A significant proportion of the population is still nomadic or semi-nomadic. The water of the area produces fine colors in the dyeing process, and the wool of the area has been considered among the finest in the rug-producing countries.

The older Kirman rugs are highly prized and a few extremely fine examples have survived from the 17th and 18th centuries. The pile was clipped short until European interests influenced rug production in the late 1800s. The western preference for longer pile, pastel colors, and French motifs was then incorporated. The centered medallion design was common, usually one medallion as the central design appearing on an all-over floral background. Carpets with animal motifs were also produced. The texture was extremely fine and had a velvet-like feel and appearance.

The rugs produced today vary dramatically in quality. The craftsmanship and dyes are not always satisfactory. It is

*careful
inspection*

therefore important to inspect carefully these new rugs before purchasing. As a general rule, an intricately woven, highly detailed carpet will be of superior quality to one with little detail, and poor resolution of design.

The most common pattern is the centered medallion placed upon an unornamented, or partially ornamented, centerfield. Less frequently, the field is covered with vines and floral designs, particularly the serrated leaf pattern.

*quick
reference*

1. Warp and Woof: Warp always cotton.

2. Pile: Almost always long.

3. Knots: Turkish and Persian.

4. Sides: Overcast.

5. Ends: Short web and fringe on both ends.

6. Sizes: Up to fifteen feet long.

7. Colors: Pastels, less frequently deep red, blue and white.

8. Miscellaneous: Kirman rugs vary greatly in quality. Some are very poor rugs, being chemically treated, loosely woven, and using poor quality dyes. These rugs are not durable, and great care should be taken to determine the quality of Kirman pieces before purchasing.

Kurdistan

Kurdistan is a province occupying the eastern part of Turkey and the western part of Iran. It is in this province that the Kurds, a nomadic people, live, raise sheep and goats, and produce fine wool and carpets. The rugs of Kurdistan are also produced by sedentary people, who depend on farming for their basic needs, and supplement their income by carpet weaving. Kurdistan is a mountainous district, through which caravans have travelled for centuries; it was, presumably, through the interchange of the travelers that the carpet industry of Kurdistan emerged.

Kurdish nomads

The Kurdish nomads, who originally wove these carpets, followed tradition and incorporated the designs used by their fathers. Little changed in hundreds of years. The antique Kurdistan carpets are rare, because they were woven solely for personal use, and not manufactured for export until the early 1900s. The designs were primarily geometric with some simple floral motifs. Goat hair was frequently used in these older rugs, but it is seldom used today.

old tradition

The newer Kurdistan carpets are manufactured for export and are readily available. The modern products are similar in design and color to the antiques, but goat hair is no longer used in their manufacture. The carpets of Kurdistan still reflect the simplicity of the antiques.

modern works

irregular designs

Generally, the designs of Kurdistan carpets are irregular figures of varying sizes, usually scattered over the center-field. The Herati and the pear motifs are occasionally used, and as a rule, the centerfield figures or designs are framed by some type of lattice pattern.

colors

Usually these rugs are woven with predominant red, green and blue. There are highlights of yellow, pink and terra cotta. One distinct feature of these rugs is that the weavers shade the colors from light to dark. The shading is similar to that seen in Chinese carpets, but not as refined.

quick reference

1. Warp and Woof: Wool or goat hair in antique rugs, cotton in modern pieces.

2. Pile: Quality wool, usually long, goat and camel hair were also used.

3. Sides: Overcast, sometimes in different colors.

4. Ends: Thick, narrow selvage with knotted fringe or loose warp ends. Usually there are one or two lines of colored wool running through the selvage. This is a Kurdish feature. Sometimes the web of one end is turned back and hemmed.

5. Sizes: Seldom large, usually around 4 x 7 feet.

Luristan

Luristan is a mountainous region southeast of Hamadan, not far from the borders of Iraq. The population was predominately nomadic, but agriculture has become more important to the area in recent years and the people are becoming more sedentary. The Luristan rugs are woven by the Luri tribe, a nomadic people who transport the rugs to Hamadan for sale.

Luri tribe

The Luri tribes originally produced the rugs for personal use in their tents. They were used as floor coverings, door hangings, sleeping mats, and as storage and saddle bags. Production was limited to personal use and for bartering purposes. Because of the small scale of manufacture, the antique rugs are scarce. The examples that have survived are similar in style and weave to the modern pieces.

saddle bags

These carpets are characteristic of most nomadic work. They have large, stylized motifs, bright colors, and multicolored fringe with colorful side overcasting. These are the most typical features of nomadic rugs. The sizes range up to about seven feet in length, and are so limited because of the continued use of horizontal looms.

typical features

Floral, animal and human motifs are the most common designs used in the centerfield of the Luristan rugs. The willow, cypress, rosettes, and Tree of Life forms are very

patterns

common as well. Smaller animal and human forms are usually secondary to the overall design. Incidentally, the animal and human forms are very stylized and almost barbaric in form, quite similar to some Caucasian pieces. The borders are decorated with stylized wavy line forms, crosses, flowers, and miscellaneous geometric forms.

colors

Bright, rich colors are features of these rugs. Brilliant red, and midnight blue usually are the predominate colors, but sometimes yellow is one of the major hues. Secondary tones include various shades of white, mustard, orange, sky blue, bright green and a chartreuse tone seldom seen in other carpets.

quick reference

1. Warp and Woof: Cotton and sometimes wool.

2. Pile: Medium to long, loosely knotted.

3. Knots: Turkish.

4. Sides: Overcast, often in multicolored yarn.

5. Ends: Colored fringe, usually with a short web.

6. Sizes: Limited to about 7 feet in length.

7. Colors: Brilliant red, deep blue, yellow, green, mustard and white.

Meshed

Meshed is an ancient city located in the district of Khorassan in northeastern Iran. For centuries Meshed has been a major center of culture and trade. Anually, thousands of pilgrims travel to this city, which is the holiest place to the Shiite Moslems. Through the centuries, pilgrams and traders have had a great influence on the carpet production of Meshed and that of the nomadic tribes and peasants of nearby areas.

holy
city

These carpets were made of very fine wool, and after years of use they developed a very deep, lustrous sheen. The pile is somewhat short and is trimmed evenly. The patterns used in the older Mesheds were usually elaborate. The pear design was frequently incorporated, was proportionately large, and was intricately embellished with floral motifs.

fine
antiques

The carpets manufactured today are quite different from those produced 100 years ago. The elaborate designs typical of the older rugs are rarely reproduced today. The current styles are comparatively simple. The wools are still excellent, and it is still possible to find an occasional rug dyed with natural dyes.

simple
design

Antique carpets of Meshed did not incorporate the centered medallion pattern which is common today. Other

animal patterns

motifs currently manufactured include almost all of the most popular and well-known Persian motifs. Animal carpets, floral motifs, and centered medallions all are used in modern rug production.

The most common colors used are rose or pink, white and blue, with accents of yellow and green. The dyes are natural in some cases, but quality synthetics are far more common today.

quick reference

1. Warp and Woof: Cotton, sometimes weft threads are dyed blue.

2. Pile: Firm and of medium length.

3. Knots: Both Persian and Turkish.

4. Sides: Overcast.

5. Ends: Web and fringe.

6. Sizes: From six to fourteen feet in length.

7. Colors: Rose, pink, blue, white, green and yellow.

Qom

Qom is a major metropolis with a population in excess of 500,000. It is located approximately seventy five miles northwest of Kashan and about one hundred miles southwest of Teheran. It is served by rail and a highway system.

major city

Carpet production began in this city approximately fifty years ago. The industry was organized specifically to provide rugs for export. Small factories were established employing up to ten weavers. The designs to be produced were diagrammed and the weavers followed these plans. Both wool and silk rugs were and are still made.

modern industry

The Qom rugs are some of the finest made in Iran today. The wool and silk are of fine quality and the craftsmanship is excellent. The rugs are densely knotted, perhaps some of the tightest currently produced, and the pile is clipped relatively short. These rugs, being so closely knotted, have a fine resolution of design.

There is no design typical of Qom rugs. The most popular Persian rug styles have been skillfully reproduced, and so examples can be seen in many patterns. Some of the rug factories of Qom will also produce rugs to desired specifications. The pattern which is the most common today is a floral-medallion style. The designs are very intricate.

made to order

colors The colors of these rugs are as varied as the styles produced. Red, blue, yellow, green, earth tones, and some pastel tones are the most typical colors.

quick reference

1. Warp and Woof: Cotton or silk.

2. Pile: Tightly knotted and cropped short.

3. Sides: Overcast.

4. Ends: Fringed, short.

5. Sizes: Usually not over seven feet in length.

6. Colors: Varied.

Sarouk

Sarouk is located at approximately 7,500 foot altitude, on the western edge of the Feraghan plain. The town is known primarily for its carpet industry. Sarouk weavers produced some of the most exquisite carpets of Persian history.

Feraghan plain

The antique Sarouk carpets are among the loveliest Persian rugs. The preparation of the wool, dyes, and foundation threads was painstaking and the craftsmanship employed was superb. The finest antique carpets are dyed in subtle tones, woven of fine, lustrous wool, and tightly knotted. Rugs dating earlier than 1870 are rare. Most of the older Sarouk carpets seen today were manufactured in factories established after this rug type achieved international popularity. The factories were organized to provide rugs for export. Hundreds of weavers were employed, and the rugs manufactured followed standard patterns.

subtle tones

Modern Sarouk carpets are still of fine quality, but not comparable to the better antiques. The wools are still carefully prepared, and the dyes are good quality synthetics. However, with the production mainly centralized in factories, the quality of craftsmanship has diminished over the years. The most common Sarouk rugs available today incorporate a large central medallion with ornamental pendants, or two or more concentric medallions on an open field.

medallion designs

cornerpieces Gracefully rendered motifs accent the medallion style rugs. Sometimes central medallion patterns are used, and at times, concentric medallions predominate. Both medallion styles usually have cornerpieces mirroring a section of the central medallion. The borders are gracefully ornamented with floral motifs, vines, etc.

colors Soft, lustrous, dark blue and red, highlights of green, olive, fawn, peach and off-white are the most common colors used today. Some Sarouk carpets available in the early 1900s were pastel in shade, often a rose tone was the primary color.

quick reference 1. Warp and Woof: Cotton.

2. Pile: Short to medium in length.

3. Knots: Persian.

4. Sides: Tightly overcast in colored wool.

5. Ends: Narrow web, some with short fringe and web.

6. Sizes: Small to room-sized carpets.

7. Colors: Blue, red, rose, green, yellow, white, buff.

Senneh

Senneh, now named Sanandaj, is a town located in northwestern Iran at approximately 5,500 feet above sea level in the province of Ardelan. This province has been one of the great rug-producing districts of Iran for centuries. The Persian knot, also called the Senneh, takes its name from this town. It is interesting, however, that this knot form is no longer used in carpets produced in the town today.

Persian knot

Antique Senneh carpets used the Persian knot form. They were woven on a foundation of cotton, wool, linen or silk. The rugs were tightly knotted with a closely clipped pile, usually less than one-half inch long. There were a limited number of styles produced. The pattern most widely produced for export was the palm design used as an all-over pattern. Some rugs had medallion designs, and these were almost always diamond-shaped and centered. The rugs typically had three border stripes, the center one wider than the other two. The border designs included roses, rosettes, and curved lines on a yellow, or less frequently, red field. The colors were subdued shades.

Modern Senneh rugs are quite similar to the antiques, although many of these newer carpets are not as tightly woven, and as mentioned, the Turkish knot is used. These carpets are very thin since the pile is still cut quite

Turkish knot

*limited
production*

short, but still they are some of the most durable of all Persian rugs. Production is limited and only two to three hundred rugs are produced annually in Senneh.

designs

The designs have changed very little over the last two hundred-year period. All-over, repeating patterns of small botahs and Herati patterns are common, although some rugs now incorporate more floral patterns. Large ornaments are seldom used, except in the pole medallion styles.

The colors used in the modern carpets are dark blue, usually as the background color, with shades of yellow, gold, green and rose. Some rugs will have a predominate yellow-green shade in place of the more typical dark blue background.

*quick
reference*

1. Warp and Woof: Cotton, wool, silk or linen.

2. Pile: Closely trimmed, thin carpet.

3. Knots: Persian in antiques, Turkish in modern.

4. Sides: Overcast with cotton or silk.

5. Ends: Selvaged on both ends, one with fringe.

6. Sizes: Usually less than eight feet, some newer rugs produced in larger sizes.

Shiraz

Shiraz is the capital city of the Province of Faristan, also called Fars. It was for a short time the capital city of Persia, from 1760 to 1779. Shiraz is primarily a marketplace for wares of local weavers, and at present, no rugs are produced in the city itself. Shiraz has a colorful history: it was at one time a major center of learning, but earthquakes have razed the elaborate structures, and the beauty immortalized by Omar Khayham is past.

capital city

The antique Shiraz rugs are generally far superior to those produced today. Many varying designs were used, including Persian floral patterns, as well as the geometric patterns typical of the Caucasian rugs. The most common pattern seen in older Shiraz rugs is the pole medallion centered on the rug, with flowers and birds scattered throughout the centerfield. Diagonal shawl stripes and small figures are often seen on the borders. The prayer rugs sometimes have a square mihrab (prayer niche) instead of the usual pointed niche.

pole medallion

The modern Shiraz carpets are not of the best quality, with the exception of the products of two nomadic tribes of the area. The two tribes producing superior carpets are the Kashkai and the Afshari tribes. Generally rug dealers will market these tribal products separately from the lesser Shiraz rugs which are not as durable, are woven from coarse wool and are loosely knotted with long pile.

tribal rugs

floral
patterns

Floral patterns including the stylized palm design and roses predominate in modern Shiraz rugs. These motifs are proportionately large compared to more finely knotted floral carpets of other districts. The pole medallion is common, and is always centered along the length of the rug. Less frequently centerfield designs of diagonal stripes and small figures are used. The background sometimes includes large stylized birds or the Tree of Life motif.

colors

Bright red contrasted with off white, and blue are the most typical color combinations. The secondary colors are various shades of yellow and mustard, some tan and earth tones. Green, a sacred color to orthodox Moslems, at times is also used.

quick
reference

1. Warp and Woof: Wool, sometimes goat hair warp, and frequently the woof is dyed red.

2. Pile: Loosely woven and somewhat coarse wool.

3. Knots: Usually Turkish, frequently more than two warp threads between rows of knots.

4. Sides: Overcast, sometimes with two or more colors, less frequently the rugs are finished with braided sides.

5. Ends: Fringed, frequently dyed.

6. Sizes: Small, area-size rugs, up to twelve feet in length.

Tabriz

Tabriz is the capital of the province of Azerbaijan, and is one of the major centers of Persian carpet production. Carpets are produced within the city as well as in the outerlying areas, but all are marketed through this major city.

Antique Tabriz carpets are ranked among some of the finest ever made. They are rare, but many museums have examples on display. The features that distinguished these carpets were their fine wool and dyes, but predominantly the excellent craftsmanship employed in their manufacture. These were tightly knotted carpets of finely spun wool, with intricate designs. The typical designs were similar to those of the Sarouk carpets, but differed in that the Tabriz did not incorporate the interlacing traceries. Their centered medallions were usually set upon a field with detailed leaves, flowers or pear patterns, but these were not interlaced as seen in the Sarouks.

fine quality

The modern Tabriz carpets are still of excellent quality. They are densely knotted, and have short to medium pile. The designs are carefully executed with the typical centered medallion style being the most common. The carpets frequently are also ornamented with floral motifs, roses, peonies and small palmettes.

modern rugs

Another style typical of Tabriz is the hunting carpet.

This style incorporates a hunting scene with dogs, horses, lions, birds and human figures in typical forest settings.

balanced patterns

Central medallions are the most common style produced today. Sometimes, one medallion sets off the central ornamentation, at other times there are a number of concentric medallions in the centerfield. However, one feature of these carpets is their symmetry. The designs of almost all Tabriz carpets are balanced; cornerpieces often imitate one quarter of the central medallion, and the borders and centerfield ornamentation reflects a well-integrated floral motif.

colors

Generally Tabriz carpets have a predominance of red, blue and ivory. The secondary colors include varying shades of the above as well as green and earth tones.

quick reference

1. Warp and Woof: Usually cotton, sometimes wool or linen in antiques.

2. Pile: Tightly knotted, short to medium in length.

3. Knots: Turkish.

4. Sides: Often double selvage.

5. Ends: Narrow web with short fringe of loose warp threads.

Yzed

Yzed is a town located south of Nain and northwest of Kirman on the western edge of the Desert of Lut. It is served by a main arterial which runs north to Teheran. The ease of transportation has been a significant influence in sustaining the rug industry, which is now primarily centered around the export market.

The carpet industry was established with weavers from Kirman, who were brought to Yzed to train local workers in the arts of dyeing, spinning, and rug weaving. The rug industry grew as the demand increased for Persian rugs, especially in the Western countries. The Yzed products resembled the Kirman rugs so closely that even experts disagree on distinguishing features. The earliest rugs resemble the Kirman products in dyes, wool and weave. The motifs included the well-known medallion pattern, sometimes with floral ornamentation in the background. There were some animal carpets, and less frequently Aubusson carpets.

Kirman influences

As these rugs so closely resemble the Kirman products, they are frequently marketed as Kirmans. It has been customary over the years to classify secondary rug types together. Hamadan rugs are such an example. All rugs produced in the outerlying districts of Hamadan are similar in weave and design, and these varying rug types are all

classification

classified and sold under one name, Hamadan. Yzed is over one hundred miles from Kirman, and it would seem illogical to apply this practice. There are two primary reasons for this: first, the rugs so closely resemble each other they are difficult to distinguish; second, the Kirman rugs have a fine reputation, are very saleable, and bring a premium on the export market.

cotton rugs

One modern rug that is easily distinguished as a Yzed is the cotton rug. This unusual product is the only hand-knotted cotton rug produced in Iran today. It is rarely exported, and examples found outside Iran have usually been purchased by tourists.

design

Centered medallion patterns are the most common, and as in the Kirman rugs, the background is frequently adorned only with cornerpieces. Other medallion styles have floral patterns covering the centerfield. Rarely are animal motifs used; these are more common to Kirman products than to Yzed work.

quick reference

1. Warp and Woof: Cotton.

2. Pile: Long in modern, short in most antiques.

3. Knots: Turkish and Persian

4. Sides: Overcast

5. Ends: Web and fringe at both ends.

6. Sizes: Up to fifteen feet long.

7. Colors: Red, blue, white and pastel shades.

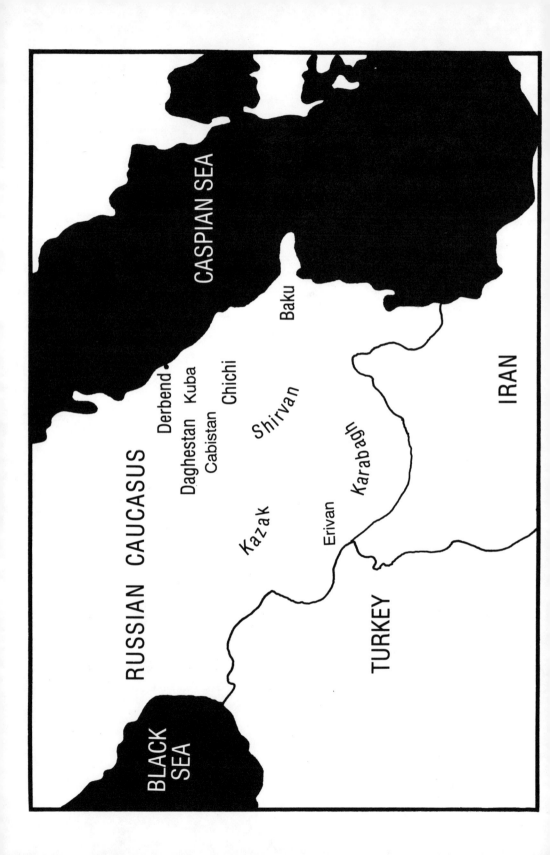

Caucasian Rugs

The country of Caucasian rugs lies between the Black and the Caspian Seas on both sides of the Caucasus Mountains, extending south to Iran and touching Turkey on the southwest. The mountain range which gives this country its name extends for seven hundred miles from the Sea of Azof to the Caspian. The Dariel pass, the only access route is flanked by 4,000 foot high cliffs. The pass is currently under Russian military jurisdiction and tightly controlled. The country is interesting and picturesque, with magnificient scenery, extensive forests, rich pasturage for sheep and large cultivated areas where food is raised for domestic consumption. Fine wool is produced and some cotton is raised. The people of this area have an ancient history. Legends abound, among them that of

Dariel pass

*wool&
cotton*

Jason and the search for the golden fleece, Colchis' stand at the foot of the Caucasus, and Prometheus' sufferings at Mount Kazbek. Wars and skirmishes proved to be a significant cultural influence so that remnants of warring tribes of various nations inhabit this country today. Alexander travelled northward to the Dariel Pass, as did Pompey and Justinian. The Turks conquered the native tribes and were later expelled under the leadership of David II, a Georgian prince. The twelfth century marks their glorious age, with Queen Tamara as their leader and idol. They succumbed to Genghis Khan, to the Persians and, last, to Russia in 1859 after a struggle of twenty years under their chief, Shamyl. Of the native people there are sixty or seventy different tribes, speaking different languages and dialects.

Queen Tamara

The art of rug-weaving was most likely transmitted from the Persians, but as the geography of the area makes travel so difficult, the textile arts have developed with little outside influence. The Caucasian rugs have a distinct character making them readily distinguishable from most Persian, Turkoman and Turkish rug types.

travel

These rugs have distinct geometric patterns on a clear ground with little or no shading. The modern Caucasian textiles, which have been only recently promoted by the Russian government after some twenty years' lapse, are almost exclusively geometric. They usually have one or more central medallions, geometric ornamentation in the

designs

centerfield, and on the borders. The colors of the finer pieces are muted tones. There are numerous Caucasian rugs currently marketed with very bright red, green and blue. However, it is generally felt that these rugs are of lesser quality than those with softer colors.

Almost every conceivable geometric form has been incorporated into the Caucasian carpets: the eight-pointed star of the Medes as well as the six-pointed star, the triangle, diamond, square, medallions of various shapes, tarantula, scorpion figures, and all-over fretwork. The "latch hook", thought to be a modification of the swastika, is a common feature of rugs of this district and on account of its almost universal use, it has been called the trademark of the Caucasian rugs. The "barber-pole" stripe which is quite similar to that in Turkoman rugs, is common to Caucasian border design. Another characteristic border design consists of motifs with saw-teeth on each side. When these are represented with alternate goblet-shaped figures, the motif is said to represent the lotus in water. The countries of the Trans-Caucasus, separated from Iran only by the river Aras, reflect at times a distinct Persian influence, especially in the use of floral designs.

barber-pole stripe

The names of the rugs of this district are not nearly as well-known as those of Persian origin. Rug making has never been as organized as in Iran and the trade routes did not exist so as to promote production for export until more recent times. Generally, the rugs were made by the people

limited production

government controls

of the area for personal use. Not until the past twenty years has Russia encouraged production of carpets for commercial purposes. For some time the government suppressed rug weaving in favor of agricultural expansion. However, today, Caucasian carpets are becoming more readily available. They are actively supported by the government, and exports have grown considerably over the recent decade.

Types of Caucasian rugs to follow:

Cabistan
Daghestan
Derbend
Chichi
Karabagh
Kasak
Malagaran
Shirvan

Vats in which Wool is Washed and Dyed

Cabistan

The district of Kuba, in the southeastern part of Daghestan, near the Caspian Sea, is the home of the Cabistan rugs. By virtue of the similarities of the people and the ease of travel between Cabistan and Daghestan, there are many similarities in the textile products of these two rug centers.

Daghestan similarities

The antique Cabistan carpets were woven primarily as grave coverings for family members. They are long, narrow rugs, from three and one half to four and one half feet wide and some up to ten feet long. These were spread between the graves of the wealthy. The rugs were of fine quality, the wool, dyes, and craftsmanship all contributed to their outstanding character. Some floral designs were used, but for the most part geometric patterns were the most common. The sides of Cabistan carpets were finished with either cotton overcasting or a selvage. The Daghestan carpets were overcast in wool and the sides were never selvaged.

excellent antiques

The modern Cabistan carpets are produced on a very limited scale, and the majority are purchased by collectors. Elongated stars woven on a plain ground with secondary motifs of all types of rectangular figures, even some small crude animal and bird designs, are the most common varieties. These rugs are woven on a cotton foundation,

elongated stars

with the pile of short, fine wool. They are somewhat longer than the Daghestan carpets, and as mentioned above, they are finished with cotton overcasting or selvaged sides.

design features

Elongated stars, rectangular figures, animals, and the centerfield filled with perpendicular stripes, the transverse rows of rectangular pear patterns forming diagonal stripes, or the ordinary fret pattern, these are all found in Cabistan carpets. The "barber pole" stripe measuring up to an inch and one half wide, is used to separate the borders, one of which invariably has large geometric motifs.

quick reference

1. Warp and Woof: Wool, but most frequently cotton.

2. Pile: Medium, not densely knotted, fine wool.

3. Knots: Turkish.

4. Sides: Overcast with cotton, sometimes selvaged.

5. Ends: Selvaged and fringed.

6. Sizes: Up to ten feet long.

7. Colors: Red, blue, ivory, green, brown.

Daghestan

Daghestan, or "mountain land," as the name translates, is an eastern province of the Caucasus, bordering on the Caspian Sea and sloping northward to the Russian steppes. The terrain is composed of deep gorges and tablelands which furnish pasturage for flocks of sheep and goats. The country is inhabited by the Lesghians, a patriarchal race, who are divided into numerous clans. These people united under Shamyl, who led the Caucasian people against Russia.

clans

Antique Daghestans are evenly and beautifully woven. Primarily these rugs were woven for devotional purposes and have been handed down from generation to generation. Thus, these rugs are extremely rare. There are a few carpets of this type displayed in museums, but it is nearly impossible to find one for sale. The rugs, are typical of most other Caucasian carpets, in featuring geometric patterns. The all-over fretwork pattern is perhaps the oldest type, but the medallion, the star and diamond motifs were also used in centerfield design. The prayer rugs incorporated a pointed prayer niche. The colors were natural tones, including beige, ivory, terra cotta, green and blue.

fretwork patterns

The modern Daghestans differ from the antique rugs in that they have a foundation of cotton warp and woof, and the dyes are synthetic. Nevertheless, they have retained

cotton warp & woof

some of the refinements of the antiques. The designs have been modified, and today are not as intricately rendered, but fine wool and careful processing have produced a fine product. The central ground, usually ivory, is covered with geometric designs of various patterns. There are usually three border stripes, with a cream-colored or light *ground* ivory ground and rectangular designs; often a reciprocal *colors* saw tooth pattern is alternated with a goblet-shaped figure. The borders are separated by lines of plain color or with the narrow twisted pattern of "barber-pole," and often bounded by Vandykes.

designs   Geometrical patterns are always used. The antiques sometimes were woven with an all-over pattern of fretwork, but the modern carpets now have open fields, often with a central medallion, and some ornamentation. Three border stripes are common and usually have patterns of latch-hook, saw-teeth and barber pole stripes.

quick 1. Warp and Woof: Antiques always used wool and the *reference* modern carpets are cotton.

2. Pile: Medium in length, not densely knotted.

3. Knots: Turkish.

4. Sides: Overcast in colored wool.

5. Ends: Narrow woven selvage with knotted fringe.

Derbend

The city of Derbend, or "fortified gate," is situated in Daghestan, on the Caspian Sea, and was for many years a military outpost of the Persians. It is a city of commercial importance, and a market for other rugs of the district, as well as a marketplace for its own products. Derbend is the largest of two towns with shipping access via the Caspian sea.

military post

The makers of the Derbend rugs were originally of the Tartar race, and their textiles reflect a strong barbaric quality. These carpets are heavier, and thicker, being more closely woven than the other carpets of the district. The designs incorporated are similar, but the Daghestan carpets have a luster which is absent in the Derbend products (which are somewhat coarse by comparison).

antique rugs

luster

The modern Derbend rugs combine Caucasian and Persian motifs. The borders have large, geometric patterns, and like the Daghestan rugs, these borders are separated by stripes of plain colors. There rugs are produced on a limited scale, primarily for export.

borders

A combination of geometric and floral motifs is used in Derbend carpets. Medallions are common, usually three medallions of equal size appearing on a dark field. Secon-

motifs

dary ornamentation includes fret-work, "latch hook" patterns, and the Persian botah and rosettes.

colors

These carpets are quite bright in appearance. The colors are rich and dynamic. Primary red is typical. Peach, green, deep blue and earth tones are also frequently incorporated together.

quick reference

1. Warp and Woof: Antiques had brown wool or goat hair, modern have white cotton.

2. Pile: Thick

3. Knots: Turkish.

4. Sides: Overcast in colored wool.

5. Ends: Fringe, or short web and knotted fringe.

6. Sizes: Up to ten feet in length.

7. Colors: Primary red, deep Persian blue, ivory, peach, green and yellow.

Chichi

Carpet weaving originated with the nomadic tribe of mountaineers, the Chichi tribe. There is some speculation that these people are descendents of the lost Jewish tribes. Rug production now is carried out in a small village north of Gandja, and only on a limited scale.

lost tribes

These rugs are an interesting combination of Caucasian and Persian styles. The typical geometric patterns of the Caucasian rugs are incorporated with the rosettes and the palm pattern of the Persian textiles. The borders, as well as the centerfield designs, incorporate both characteristics. Another feature distinguishing these carpets is their shape. Most of the antique carpets are nearly square in shape, to approximately six feet in length. Also, there are rare examples with an all-over repeating pattern, which is an unusual feature in any carpets from the Caucasus regions.

antique rugs

shape

The designs are still carefully rendered and unlike any other Caucasian rug, the design may cover the entire field in a repeating pattern. There are geometric and floral motifs displayed throughout the centerfield in dark, yet rich, colors. Often there are six to eight borders, with one being the largest and centered between the remaining secondary borders. These borders are always highly ornamented, and rosettes often appear in the secondary stripes. Frequently the rectangular figures running diagonally to the border stripes distinguish the Chichi rugs.

design

A combination of geometric and floral motifs is typical of these rugs. The Persian rosette pattern is frequently interspersed with rectangular, square and octagonal motifs. These rugs are intricately woven, with little or no unadorned areas. Usually, the entire centerfield is covered with small, sometimes repeating patterns.

colors

The colors are usually dark and, whereas many Caucasian products use a light centerfield color, the Chichi carpets usually have a deep blue or brown background and lighter shades are used only in the borders. The basic colors used are red, blue, brown, tan, and ivory.

quick reference

1. Warp and Woof: Wool and cotton.

2. Pile: Fairly dense, fine wool, medium in length.

3. Knots: Turkish.

4. Sides: Finished as the Daghestan carpets with colored overcasting.

5. Ends: Narrow woven selvage with knotted fringe.

6. Sizes: Nearly square from four by five feet to five by six feet.

Karabagh

This carpet district is the most southerly province of the
Caucasus, and for hundreds of years it has been influenced
by the Persian carpet-producing districts bordering it.
Karabagh has no port city and so its products have been
marketed to the north through Baku or exported along the
trade routes to the south. The textile industry has been in
existence for centuries, and its products have, over the
years, reflected the influence of the European as well as
the Persian tastes.

The antique rugs of this district often reflect the foreign
influences that were in vogue at the time. There are
numerous examples of the large floral motifs that were so
popular in the French household in the 1800s, and, of
course, the various designs that were perfected in the
Persian textiles, which include Herati patterns, botahs
and varying forms of medallions. However, there are a few
distinguishing features of the rugs: (1) They were manufactured entirely of wool, (2) The designs were larger and
somewhat less intricate than the Persian styles imitated,
(3) The carpets were generally long and narrow, and (4)
The background color was dark.

The rugs currently produced in this province reflect similar characteristics to the antiques. The craftsmanship varies somewhat from one city to another, but overall, these

rugs are durable and made of quality wool. Some are similar to Daghestan carpets, but, generally the colors are not as bright. Also, many patterns have been imitated, from both Persian origin, Caucasian, and French.

designs

The designs used in these carpets are extremely diverse. Bokhara type patterns have been used, as well as the geometric Caucasian medallions, stars, diamonds and stylized animal figures. As this province was under Persian rule, these carpets incorporated designs more typical of Persian rugs than have any other products of the Caucasus. The Persian motifs, however, are large and less intricate than those in Persian rugs.

quick reference

1. Warp and Woof: Wool.

2. Pile: Medium in length.

3. Knots: Turkish.

4. Sides: Overcast.

5. Ends: Short fringe at both ends.

6. Sizes: Usually long and narrow.

7. Colors: Modern have darker background colors than the antiques; red, yellow and green tones are common.

Kasak

In the district of Erivan, near Lake Goktcha, and in sight of Mount Ararat, live the nomad and semi-nomadic Kasak tribes of the Caucasus. Their origin is unknown but they are related to the Cossacks of Russia. Many are shepherds, living a semi-nomadic existence, travelling to the mountains in the summer months, and south in the winter.

tribal heritage

Of all the carpets of the Caucasus, the Kasak rug is possibly the most identifiable: its main characteristic is the predominance of geometric designs. This is especially noticeable in the antique rugs where the designs are large, bold and distinct. The centerfield is somewhat open with large symmetrically-placed medallions and secondary ornamentation along the outside of the centerfield. The colors are equally distinctive. Few colors are incorporated into one carpet: red and brown are almost always used along with some beige, green and terra cotta.

limited colors

Kasak carpets are the most plentiful carpets available today from the Caucasus region. However, the quality is not consistent; there are two types exported, one being preferable. The finer of these two classes features more muted coloring. Red, terra cotta, green, ivory, brown, and tan are the most common colors used today in the better rugs.

motifs   Geometric motifs are the hallmark of this carpet type.
Large central medallions on a sparingly ornamented field
are the most common style. Kasak carpets generally have
one or three central medallions, with secondary ornamentation of the barber pole, latch hook and fretwork. The
designs are usually symmetrical and well-integrated. Open
areas in the centerfield contrast gracefully with the fea-
tured designs.

Red, deep blue, green, yellow, terra cotta, brown and
ivory are the colors most frequently used in Kasak rugs.
The colors are never shaded. One feature of these carpets
is the elegant contrast of colors harmonizing with the
usually large, geometric motifs.

quick   1. Warp and Woof: Cotton.
reference

2. Pile: Medium in length.

3. Knots: Turkish.

4. Sides: Overcast in colored wool.

5. Ends: Web and fringe.

6. Sizes: Up to about seven feet in length.

7. Colors: Red, blue, ivory, green, brown, yellow.

Malagran

In this area, as is true for many districts of the Caucasus, there are many distinct tribes and peoples, most of whom have a history of rug weaving. From one of these rug producing districts, not far to the west of the Tchetchens, comes a rug called the Malagran. It is of a type which is distinctly of the Daghestan family, but with features that distinguish it from the other carpets of the area.

The features that distinguish this type of carpet are: first, the size - they are small, from about three to four feet in length and from two to two feet six inches in width; second, they are made of quality wool which takes more of a luster than the ordinary Daghestan; third, the warp and woof are made of white, hard-twisted wool, which forms the selvage and is woven into a narrow web at the ends with a fringe tied in knots.

distinguishing features

It seems that there are few Malagran carpets exported today. They are still manufactured, but the industry has not prospered as have other carpet-producing districts in the Caucasus.

few exports

One of the most common patterns of the Malagran rugs is a field covered with octagons. These are placed in such a way as to give a latch-hook effect. In the center of the octagons are stars, squares, or small tree-shaped figures.

octagon

design   There are usually three borders, nearly all of the same width, and separated by a twisted stripe. The patterns do vary, however, as some also will have floral motifs which are similar to stylized Persian rosette patterns. The outer-.most border usually is ornamented with rhomboids, flowers or a modified latch hook design.

The colors of these carpets are primarily rich red, blue, tawny yellow and brown. The colors are incorporated in such a way as to contrast with the designs. They are colorful carpets, but not brassy in appearance.

quick   1. Warp and Woof: Wool.
reference

2. Pile: Loosely woven, medium in length.

3. Knots: Turkish.

4. Sizes: Woven selvage of white wool.

5. Ends: Narrow web with knotted fringe at both ends.

6. Sizes: Small, up to four feet long.

7. Colors: Rich red, blue, tawny yellow and brown.

Shirvan

Shirvan is a carpet-producing district located in the southern Caucasus region, more accurately termed as part of the Transcaucasus. Baku is the largest city, and as it is located on the Caspian Sea, it is the major city of export for all of the carpets produced in the landlocked areas of this district. Geographically, Shirvan is separated from Daghestan by the main range of the Caucasus mountains. It provides excellent pasturage for sheep and goats, and cotton production has proven to be very successful.

location

Carpet production for export did not begin until the early 1900s at which time the Shirvan carpet was produced in large quantities. The carpets produced in the 1800s and earlier were generally small in size, no larger than 5 feet in length. The wools were very fine, as were the natural dyes. The patterns were distinctly Caucasian, as is still true today, but with some Persian influence reflected in the floral and vine motifs. The centerfields of Shirvan rugs were covered most typically with geometric forms, medallions, diamonds and stars. They were very colorful, using highly contrasting tones of blue, red, green, and brown, usually on an ivory field.

*recent
exports*

The modern Shirvan carpets are similar to the antiques in design, however, the wool is coarser and the nap longer. The borders are probably the most distinctive feature of these rugs, especially as a key in distinguishing them from

*longer
pile*

serrated leaf

other carpet types. The borders number three to five with one primary stripe as well as a secondary stripe of nearly equal size. The serrated leaf and wine glass patterns are used extensively in border design. The pear motif, botah and carnation are also frequently used in the intricately rendered borders. Another feature which distinguishes Shirvan carpets is the use of a broad spectrum of colors. The Shirvan rugs incorporate brighter tones, and usually more colors into one piece than is true for other Transcaucasian products.

patterns

It is nearly impossible to enumerate all of the patterns currently used in the manufacture of Shirvan carpets. All types of medallions are used as well as stylized floral and animal motifs. The centerfields are ornamented with smaller Caucasian motifs, and the borders are distinctive with usually two border stripes of equal size and the remaining stripes narrower. The borders often have the barber pole stripes and the latch hook pattern.

quick reference

1. Warp and Woof: Modern always cotton, antiques sometimes wool.

2. Pile: Short to medium in length.

3. Knots: Turkish.

4. Sides: Overcast web selvage and sometimes overcast.

5. Ends: Web, with one or both having knotted fringe

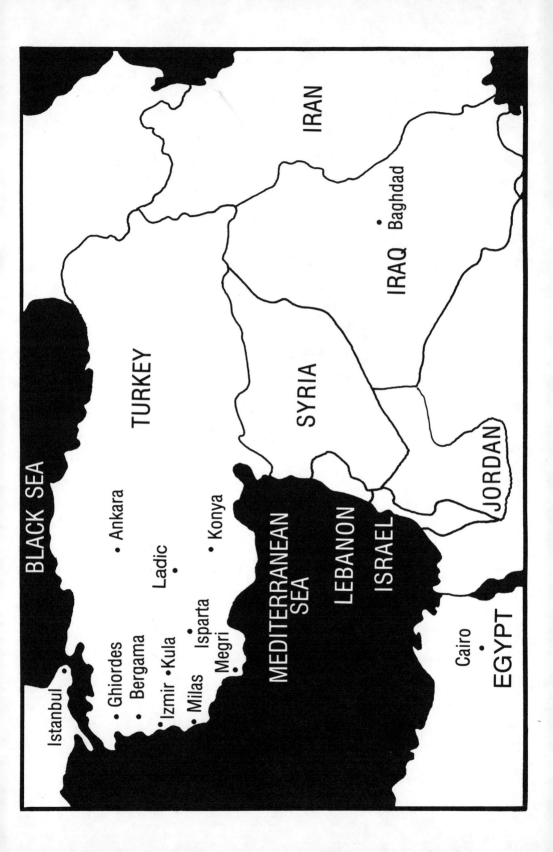

Turkish Rugs

Asia
Minor

The country of the Turkish rugs is the district of Asia
Minor, or as the Greeks termed it, Anatolia, the "land of
the sunrise." It is an area rich in history: the land of the
Iliad and Homer; the home of early Greek civilization,
with its arts, industries, and commerce, supplanted in
succession by Persian, Roman, and Turkish rule. The
early apostolic churches have been supplanted by
Islam. Islam is the major religion in Turkey. This
district is about the size of France, a very fertile table land,
surrounded by mountain ranges, with valleys sloping to
the Black Sea on the north and to the Mediterranean on
the west and south. Its natural resources, under Turkish
rule, are being developed and still some of the finest grades
of wool for rug making are produced in quantities, as well

fine
wools

as mohair from the angora goat, silk, cotton, linen, and dye-stuffs.

people

Its people are diverse. There are many Greeks of pure lineage, Kurds, partly sedentary, and partly nomadic shepherds, Turkomans of the mountain districts of the Taurus, Armenians, and some Europeans. With the exception of the cities like Smyrna, Broussa, and Adana, where European influence is strong, the life in the rural areas is still somewhat primitive.

rug production

In very few parts of this area is rug-weaving carried out in the old style, where one family raises, cards and spins the wool, makes the dyes and weaves the carpet. Factories have been established for the manufacture of carpets, where hundreds of weavers are employed, much in the same way as in the Iranian factories. Primarily the work force includes women and children, though, with stricter control on the part of the government, child labor is not as extensive as earlier in this century.

The materials for rug-making are of the best quality. The wool of this area, much of which is raised by Turkoman tribes, is of fine quality, and is spun loosely, giving a fluffy appearance and producing a soft blending of colors. An

spinning machines

attempt to introduce spinning machines failed in the early 1920s; however, with industrialization of the rug industry taking hold, hand-spun wool is becoming rare. The Angora goat furnishes a fine grade of mohair, which produces a rug with a beautiful sheen when new; but with wear, this rug becomes matted and dull, and wears more readily than does wool. Silk and cotton are both raised in abundance and are used for clothing and rugs.

silk & cotton

For a time inferior synthetic dyes were used extensively in Turkoman rugs, especially around the 1920s when they supplanted natural dyes throughout Iran and India. Today, synthetic dyes still predominate, but they are of good quality and produce natural-looking colors that are colorfast. Red, a favorite color in Turkoman rugs, is still at times taken from madder, a plant which grows abundantly throughout the East.

dyes

List of Turkish rugs to follow:

Bergama
Ghiordes
Kula
Ladic
Milas
Yuruk
Oushak

Turkish Girls At The Loom

Bergama

Bergama, once known as Pergamon, is one of the old Greek cities of Asia Minor. It is located approximately forty miles northeast of Izmir. The carpets produced here have a distinctive Caucasian feel, and have been represented in many famous Holbein paintings.

These are very scarce and highly prized rugs. They are distinctly different from any other type of Turkish carpet, and more easily confused with Caucasian rugs than those of Turkish origin. They usually have a medallion design, with the field covered with geometric patterns. The borders have wide floral panels, frequently with a background of a contrasting tone to that of the centerfield. The texture is very soft, and with age the wool has taken on a very lustrous sheen.

The modern Bergama carpets are popular, and are currently produced in many sizes. They still display the large, geometric motifs typical of Caucasian work, yet they can be easily distinguished. The designs are similar, but the texture of the Bergama is much thicker, and the pile is longer than the Caucasian products. The sides are also finished with a flat selvage, frequently with a band of color, or some floral motif woven into the selvage. Sometimes the fringe is braided into several strands with a bead or charm fastened to it.

*key
patterns*

Large geometric motifs are a feature of these rugs. Medal-lions,in various shapes are a central feature, always appearing on a highly ornamented field. The key pattern is frequently used in the center field, as are geometric floral motifs. The borders have one central stripe, usually three times as wide as the adjacent stripes.

colors

Bright, contrasting colors are typical of these rugs. Many shades of blue are often incorporated into one piece, with tones ranging from light sky blue to deep indigo. Red, yellow, green, ivory, white, terra cotta and blue-green are also used. But, the predominate color of most Bergama carpets is red, the secondary color is blue, and highlights always incorporate some ivory or white.

*quick
reference*

1. Warp and Woof: Cotton.

2. Pile: Thick and long.

3. Knots: Turkish.

4. Sides: Selvaged.

5. Ends: Selvaged, sometimes fringed.

6. Sizes: Vary.

7. Colors: Red, blue, white, yellow, green, terra cotta.

Ghiordes

Approximately fifty miles northeast of Izmir (Smyrna) is the ancient city of Ghiordes. This is the most famous carpet-producing city of Turkey, where the finest prayer rugs originated, and after which the Turkish knot was named. Carpet production has continued uninterrupted since the early 1600s.

Turkish knot

It has been said that the finest prayer rugs originated from this town. Examples made as early as the 17th century are preserved in museums and in private collections throughout the world. These rugs are highly prized, and considered by many experts to rival the perfection of the finest Persian creations. One feature of these prayer rugs is that the niche is frequently of one color, which appears in striking contrast to the intricate ornamentation that covers the remaining field. The mihrab in the antique examples was always supported by two columns, whereas in the modern pieces, this is an unusual feature.

prayer niche

Prayer rugs are the major textile product of this town today. Production is geared for export, and unfortunately, the craftsmanship is not always of good quality. The motifs of the prayer rugs have changed somewhat to include floral motifs which have, for the most part, replaced the columns in the antique pieces.

major product

spandrels   Intricate designs are a feature of these rugs. Often the spandrels above the point of the mihrab are filled with arabesque work or with floral motifs. The central panel sometimes has a frieze at the top and bottom. The borders have narrow stripes enclosing them. The designs are frequently realistic floral patterns or stylized rosettes and palm patterns. Seldom in these rugs are the floral motifs connected by wavy lines as are Persian floral rugs.

color   One tone generally predominates in the Ghiordes rugs. Contrasting colors highlight the intricate designs, but the colors are harmonious, though bright. Green, blue, yellow, ivory or red red are the most frequently-used colors in the modern pieces.

quick
reference
1. Warp and Woof: Cotton, sometimes silk and linen.

2. Pile: Medium in length, soft wool.

3. Knots: Turkish.

4. Sides: Sometimes with silk selvage, but usually wool.

5. Ends: Fringe, or web and fringe.

6. Sizes: Prayer rug sizes up to room-size carpets.

7. Colors: Red, blue, green, yellow and ivory.

Kula

Southeast of Ghiordes, and due east of Izmir, is Kula, one of the old rug-weaving districts of Turkey. Prayer rugs were its finest products, and its sole textile output until the demand in foreign markets encouraged production of larger, room-sized carpets. There are many similarities between the antique Ghiordes and the antique Kula prayer rugs, making it difficult at times for experts to distinguish between the two.

large carpets

These rugs are highly prized, though possibly not as greatly as the finest Ghiordes rugs. The two products differ slightly in that the knotting is not as dense in the Kula rugs, and the colors vary somewhat. The prayer arch is less sharp than that of the Ghiordes. When columns support the prayer niche, they are generally not as architecturally exact, and the floral motifs are not as intricate as in the Ghiordes rugs.

antique rugs

The current production of carpets has sustained itself to meet the growing export market. Factories have been organized, and carpets as well as prayer rugs are currently produced, primarily for export. The quality of these carpets, as is true for the Ghiordes, reflects the commercial trend and quality has been sacrificed for increased production. Modern products are available in prayer rug sizes up to about 12 feet in length. They are somewhat loosely

factory production

woven with medium-length pile of quality wool. They are woven on a cotton foundation, and are fairly durable, and

cost

less costly than most Persian rugs of similar size.

The centerfield in the prayer rugs, instead of being plain, as in the Ghiordes, has a floral pattern extending through

design

it. The temple design has less architectural precision, and the arch is frequently serrated. Sometimes there is a point at both ends, and the rug is then designated as a hearth rug. The borders in the hearth rugs usually have many narrow ribbon stripes, alternating light and dark. The borders in the prayer rugs are fewer in number, usually three.

quick reference

1. Warp and Woof: Cotton.

2. Pile: Medium to long.

3. Knots: Turkish, loosely woven.

4. Sides: Overcast.

5. Ends: Fringe.

6. Sizes: Prayer rug to room sized carpets.

7. Colors: Red, blue, green, brown and ivory.

Ladic

Ladic is a town located north of the ancient capital city of
Konya (Konieh). Sheep and goats provide the primary
source of income for the people in and around the town,
but technological advancements are encouraging the de-
velopment of agriculture, and as a result the economic
priorities are slowly changing.

agriculture

Prayer rugs and small mats were produced in Ladic. These
rugs were made of very finely-spun wool. The colors were
somewhat unusual compared to other Turkish prayer rugs,
with characteristic tones of green, red, blue and ivory.
The patterns were Turkish, but adapted to smaller sur-
faces. A distinguishing feature of the prayer rugs was the
use of the inverted pomegranate motif, which appeared in
rows of three or more below the prayer niche. The Rho-
dian lily frequently formed a border stripe and the Van-
dyke motif was commonly used.

*antique
rugs*

*tones &
patterns*

The Ladic rugs produced today are inferior quality textiles.
The wool is coarse, and somewhat stiff, and the dyes used
are synthetic or poor-quality natural dyes. The quality of
craftsmanship has been lost. The weaving is quite loose,
and the designs are crude.

*coarse
wool*

The patterns mentioned above are still used, but rarely
now are the rugs woven tightly enough to produce clear,

intricate patterns. The prayer rugs have an unusual style of mihrab, which has one obliquely pointed dome with a triangular dome on either side.

dyes

The Ladic dyes of the late 1800s and earlier were interesting, particularly the red dye color which was bright, rich, and deep, with a bluish tone. Indigo, deep sky blue, ivory and yellow highlights were colors frequently used. Today red, yellow, blue and tan are common.

quick reference

1. Warp and Woof: Wool in the antiques, cotton in modern

2. Pile: Short and closely knotted in antiques, long and loosely knotted in modern.

3. Knots: Turkish.

4. Sides: Narrow web.

5. Ends: Narrow web with fringe.

6. Sizes: Prayer rugs up to three by seven, mats up to two feet square; modern rugs are also produced in larger sizes.

7. Colors: Magenta red, deep sky blue, ivory, yellow.

Milas

Milas is a small town located southeast of Kula, not far from the island of Rhodes. It is inland yet has received influences from foreign cultures throughout history. Rug-production, originally, was centered around devotional purposes. Today, however, production is limited to a handful of families and no rugs are produced for export.

limited production

Milas, or Carian rugs have been produced for centuries, but the height of the textile form was reached in the 18th and 19th centuries. Primarily the rugs made during these periods were prayer rugs, measuring up to six or seven feet in length, and approximately two to three feet wide. The designs resemble the Ladic prayer rugs, and the Milas, similar to Ladic coloring, have an unusual magenta red. One peculiar feature of Milas prayer rugs is what has been called the "thumb print pattern" which is usually an outer border motif with a pattern similar to adjacent thumb prints, or a rounded saw-tooth pattern. The niche is proportionally small to that of other Turkish prayer rugs. The remaining space is taken up by border stripes, often numbering ten or fifteen. These stripes are of varying widths, usually each with its individual pattern. Rosettes, and other stylized floral motifs are frequently used in the border designs, as is the saw-tooth pattern, the tree of life and miscellaneous geometric forms. The color-tone of these carpets is generally light, with extensive use of a

history

saw-tooth pattern

yellow-green color, uncommon to all other Turkish rugs. White was frequently used as a background color, and red, blue, green, and earth tones completed the spectrum.

No carpets are produced today for export from the town of Milas. There are still some families that have carried on the art form, but their products are very limited and not commercially exported. The antique Milas carpets are rare, and the modern carpets virtually nonexistent.

rare antiques

colors

There are two colors peculiar to Milas prayer rugs; one is a very unusual blue-red tone, akin to that of the magenta in Ladic prayer rugs, the other is a yellow-green, not found in any other Turkish carpets. The color scheme in these rugs is more limited than that used in Ladic rugs, but includes a deep blue shade, brown, yellow and hints of green.

quick reference

1. Warp and Woof: Wool.

2. Pile: Thick and medium in length.

3. Knots: Turkish.

4. Sides: Selvaged.

5. Ends: Colored selvage and fringe.

6. Sizes: Prayer rug size only.

7. Colors: Yellow-green, magenta, blue, ivory and brown.

Yuruk

The word "Yuruk" translates as wanderer and, as would be expected, the rugs of this type are made by nomad tribes. The Yuruk tribes resemble the Turkoman people, and possibly they are descendants of tribes stranded in Turkey after an invasion. Originally, these tribes lived in oblong tents, made of black goat hair. Their summers were passed in the Taurus Mountains and their winters in the fertile plains of Cilicia, near the warm Mediterranean coast.

nomad tribes

A feature of Anatolian, or Turkish, carpets is their texture. They generally have a fluffy pile and are loosely woven in comparison to most Persian carpets. These features are present in the Yuruk rugs, but the traditional Turkish designs were never used. The motifs characteristic of these rugs are more akin to the Kasak tribes of the Caucasus. The large, bold, geometric motifs were central to the carpet's designs. Brilliant, contrasting colors, similar to those of some Kasak rugs were also used by the Yuruks. However, the weave was traditionally Turkish with a thick, lustrous and loosely knotted pile. The wool used was very fine, and with use it took on a splendid luster. The rug, as a whole, often had a sort of metallic brilliancy. The finish of the antique Yuruk rugs is in keeping with the majority of Turkish textiles, having a colored selvage and fringe braided into rough cords.

texture

design similarities

unevenly clipped

The modern carpets are somewhat primitive in style. They have a longer pile than the antiques, they are unevenly clipped and loosely knotted. The motifs are generally large and a bit irregular. Medallions are central to most patterns, and frequently two or more appear in the centerfield with complementary diamonds, stars and various other geometric shapes ornamenting the background and borders.

design

The modern rugs have geometric ornamentation, which is typical of almost all Turkish carpets. Diamonds, stars, hexagons, rectangles, octagons, cross patterns, and triangles predominate in the Yuruk textiles. The designs are generally large, and not intricately woven.

quick reference

1. Warp and Woof: Wool, cotton or goat hair.

2. Pile: Wool, loosely knotted, long, unevenly clipped.

3. Knots: Turkish.

4. Sides: Web or overcast.

5. Ends: Web sometimes with braided fringe.

6. Sizes: Up to seven feet in length.

7. Colors: Ususally red or blue predominates, highlights of olive green, yellow, ivory and brown.

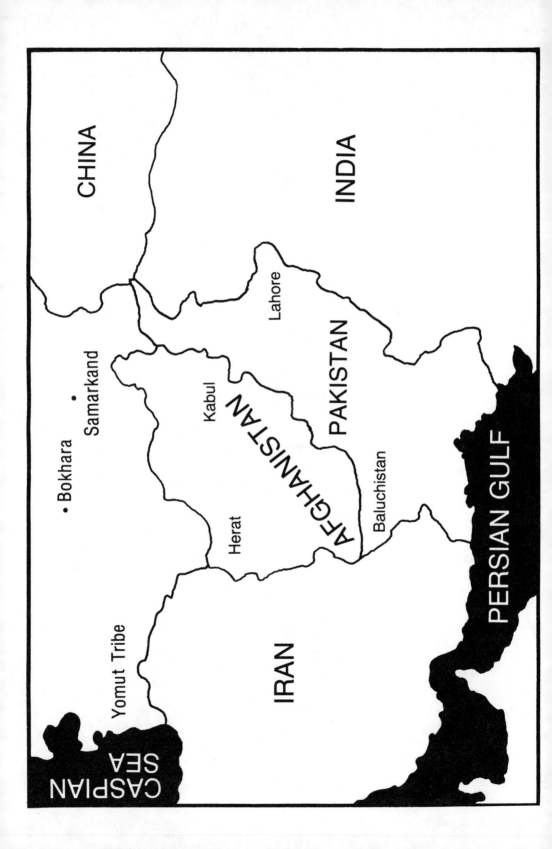

Turkoman Rugs

The rugs of Central Asia, or the Turkoman rugs, include those of the Turkoman tribes of Russian Turkestan. The Bokhara or Tekke, the Afghan, and the Yomud and Baluchi rugs are all included in this category. Samarkand rugs are a mixture of Turkoman and Chinese. Here, in this volume, the Samarkand rugs are included under Chinese classification.

types of Turkomans

Central Asia is bordered on the west by the Caspian Sea. In the south it borders Iran, and in the east, China. This area is primarily desert, with some fertile tablelands and scattered oases. For centuries nomadic tribes have continuously migrated to avoid the hardships of droughts, icy storms, and blistering heat. Sheep, goats and some other

geography

livestock are raised in the area. There is some farming, but the growing season is short and without irrigation and

agriculture limited

machinery, agricultural productivity is low. Cotton is one of the crops raised on a limited scale. It is grown for use in rugs and for clothing. Dye stuffs are not cultivated as many of the plants are indigenous and grow in sufficient quantity to provide ample sources for rug production.

The carpets of this area, and the saddle bags, tent strips, and mats look remarkably similar at first glance. The color scale and the motifs are more limited than those of the Persian or Caucasian textiles. Generally, the Turkoman

geometric patterns

rugs are distinguished by geometric patterns, repeating throughout the centerfield. The colors are rich tones of deep red, blue, brown, and a golden tan. These rugs are tightly knotted, unlike most other nomadic carpets, and they are usually made with the Persian knot. The pile is thick and resilient, and is clipped to a medium length or quite short depending on the rug type.

Types of Turkoman rugs to follow:

Afghan
Bokhara
Baluchi
Yomud

Girls at the Loom

Afghan

The country of the Afghan rugs is that part of Afghanistan bordering on Russian Turkestan. The country is a wild and rugged one, where still, bandits are not uncommon. To-day, the majority of carpets are produced in towns where small factories have been organized. The rugs are marketed through Kabul and some through Moscow.

wild country

The antique Afghan rugs were made in larger sizes than other Turkoman products. This was the result of early Western influence which encouraged production for export in the early 1800s. Because of this early organization of the rug industry, there are more antique Afghan rugs available than any other Turkoman rug type. The Afghan rugs are recognized at once as belonging to the Turkoman family. They incorporate the octagon motif, typical red and blue tones, but their texture is much heavier. They are of coarser weave and have a longer pile than other Turkoman rugs.

Rug-production has grown steadily in the last decade. The government has encouraged the industry, but with the current political upheavals there is some uncertainty as to its future.

political upheavals

The rugs resemble the antiques with a more loosely-knotted and even longer pile than the rugs made up until

knotting

the late 1800s. They are woven of durable, quality wool, either on a cotton or wool foundation. The pattern is geometric. The typical Afghan octagon is square in shape, sometimes it is called the "elephant foot" motif or the Afghan gul.

elephant foot motif

The "elephant foot" pattern is the square octagon motif just described. The typical motif is used as a repeating pattern, symmetrically arranged in rows over the center-field of the rug. The borders are not as predominate a feature as in the Afghan antiques. The border ornamentation occupies no more than one quarter of the rug's surface in the modern pieces.

quick reference

1. Warp and Woof: Wool, cotton, some antiques were goat hair.

2. Pile: Sometimes up to one inch long.

3. Knots: Persian and Turkish

4. Sides: Selvaged and sometimes overcast.

5. Ends: Web with fringe.

6. Colors: Red, brown, blue, yellow and ivory.

Bokhara

The Bokhara, or more properly, the Tekke rugs are made by the Tekke Turkoman tribes who inhabit the country extending southwest of the city of Bokhara to Afghanistan and to the Khorassan Province in Iran. These tribes of nomad Turkomans were forcibly subdued by the Russians under the direction of General Skobeleff. Thousands died in the struggle until their surrender in 1899. Thousands of carpets are now made annually for export. These are marketed through the city of Bokhara.

Russian control

There are few Bokhara carpets which date back to the early 1800s or before. Most examples that exist today are estimated to have been made in the mid- to late 1800s. Since carpets were not produced for export, only for use in the nomadic tents, few have survived. Those rugs that have survived, however, are extremely difficult to date precisely and experts can only roughly estimate their age. The designs, techniques of weave, and dyes, have changed very little from these early examples.

few antique examples

Bokharas are some of the most recognizable rugs of the Orient, possibly second only to Chinese carpets. The designs are repeating geometric forms, which cover the entire centerfield of the piece. The borders generally encompass approximately one third of the rug's area, and again use various geometric patterns as ornamentation.

many sizes   The sizes vary from small mats up to sixteen feet in length. Since the nomadic tribes lived in small tents, which would not accommodate larger carpets, the room-sized Bokharas are a recent innovation. These rugs have been produced only in response to foreign demand.

design   A form of the octagon pattern is the most typical design used in Bokhara rugs. It is usually arranged in rows which cover the centerfield. Depending on the size of the rug, there are from two to five rows across and from three to fifteen rows down. The borders, one or two primary, and three or more secondary, also display repeating geometric motifs. Border designs rarely display the octagon, more typically the following are used: tarantula, diamond and cross motifs.

quick reference   1. Warp and Woof: Cotton.

2. Pile: Dense and clipped short.

3. Knots: Persian.

4. Sides: Overcast.

5. Ends: Web and fringe, some carpets have a long web on each end.

6. Sizes: Two feet up to sixteen feet in length.

7. Colors: Wine red, deep blue, tan, brown, ivory.

Baluchi

The Baluchi rugs, as one might not expect, are produced hundreds of miles north of the Baluchistan province in Pakistan. The nomad weavers live in Russian-controlled areas bordering Iran and the Khorassan province.

The antique rugs were always made in small sizes (a feature of nomadic wares) on a wool foundation with coarse wool pile, some camel and goat hair, but never with silk. The designs of these early rugs combined traditional Turkoman geometric patterns with motifs adapted from Persian rugs. These adapted motifs include the tree of life, floral designs and the botah. The Baluchi renderings of these motifs, however, are readily distinguished because they are stylized to geometric proportions.

The rugs woven by the Baluchi tribes differ today from the earlier works in that the foundation is usually cotton, the dyes are frequently synthetic and the use of camel hair is waning. The sizes are still small, though, usually measuring around three to five feet in length. The designs are similar to those of the antiques, as they still combine Turkoman geometric forms with stylized Persian motifs. The texture of these rugs is heavy and somewhat coarse. They have proven to be exceptionally durable rugs, and still are available at reasonable prices.

floral patterns

The designs of these nomadic rugs are always geometric. The borders display motifs typical of other Turkoman wares, including the octagon, diamond shapes, etc. But the centerfield will most frequently incorporate rigid floral patterns, some bird motifs, the botah and tree of life patterns. Additionally, the centerfield designs are not as rigidly symmetrical as for example, the Bokhara patterns. The Baluchi weavers will at times, have a random pattern of floral motifs scattered throughout the centerfield.

color

The predominating colors are typically deep red and a dark blue, with the background frequently in a camel color, as seen in Hamadan rugs. Secondary colors include ivory, green, brown, yellow and sometimes black.

quick reference

1. Warp and Woof: Cotton in modern.

2. Pile: Thick and coarse.

3. Knots: Persian.

4. Sides: Overcast and selvaged.

5. Ends: Web and fringe.

6. Sizes: Up to about five feet in length.

7. Colors: Deep red, blue, camel, brown, yellow, ivory and green.

Yomud

Southwest of the Bokhara rug district, bordering on the Caspian Sea and north of the Khorassan province in Iran, live the Yomud tribes. These tribes are semi-nomadic. Herds of sheep and goats are raised and some crops are cultivated on the fertile tablelands north of Bokhara. Rug production is growing under the encouragement of the Russian government, and the majority of the products are exported to western countries.

fertile tablelands

These rugs are scarce, and as with the Bokhara rugs, examples earlier than the 19th century are virtually unknown. There are a few pieces in museum and private collections, but rarely are these offered for sale. The patterns and colors of the Yomud rugs are quite similar to the Bokhara rugs. Repeating geometric forms on the centerfield, with geometric borders are typical. Their characteristic octagon or 'gul' pattern is proportionately different from that of the Bokhara rugs. The Yomud octagon motif is almost twice as wide as it is high, more elongated than in Bokhara rugs.

antique rugs

similar to Bokhara

Yomud rugs are very popular in the west and production has increased in response to meet the expanding export market. They are available in sizes ranging up from two feet to nine feet in length. Similar to the Bokharas, their color schemes usually include no more than three hues in

expanding production

one piece. The designs are geometric with proportionately smaller border stripes than the Bokhara. These durable rugs are made of quality wool with Persian knots.

motif

The rugs resemble other Turkoman products in color, texture, and end finish, but are distinguished in design. The diamond with a "latch hook" ornamentation is a frequent motif. When the octagon occurs it is more elongated than in the Tekke rugs. The borders have geometric figures with the latch hook on an ivory ground, and frequently a narrow "barber pole" stripe is used to frame the centerfield and border stripes.

color

The colors of the Yomud rugs are not a distinguishing feature, compared to other Turkoman products at least. However, the red is somewhat darker, and duller than that seen in the Bokharas, almost a brown red tone.

quick reference

1. Warp and Woof: Cotton or wool.

2. Pile: Densely knotted, short pile.

3. Knots: Persian.

4. Sides: Overcast, sometimes selvaged.

5. Ends: Web and fringe.

6. Sizes: Two feet up to nine feet in length.

7. Colors: Brick red, blue, brown, gold and ivory.

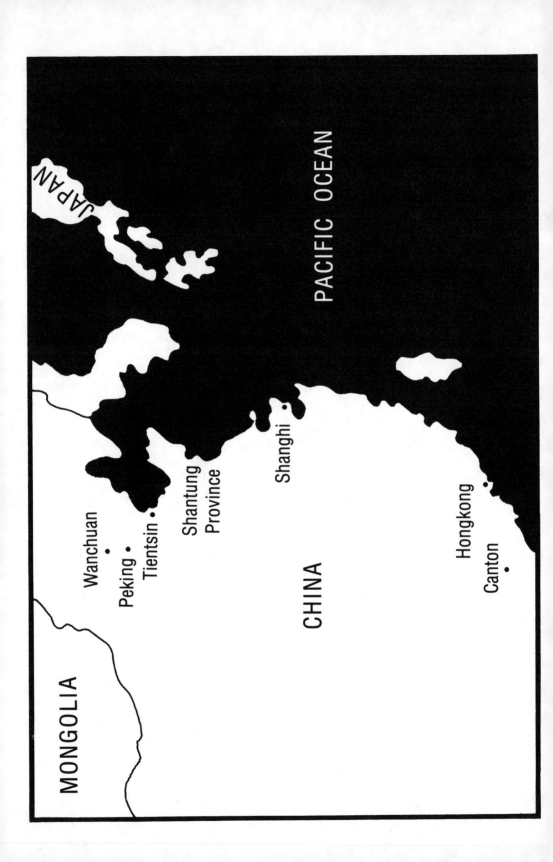

Chinese Rugs

China is the home of the oldest continuing nation dating back in recorded history to 2852 B.C. The dynasties in China were the patrons of the arts, and, as a result, some of the world's finest porcelains, bronzes and textiles were produced. The arts of China were strongly influenced by the religious philosophies. Buddhism, Taoism and Confucianism are the three that had the greatest influence. Taoism and Confucianism are native, whereas Buddhism spread to China from India. Buddhism, being rich in symbols, provided a wealth of motifs for the textile products of China. The lotus, a symbol of purity, is frequently seen in the porcelains, bronzes, paintings, embroideries and carpets of China. Other Buddhist symbols include two fish, the knot of eternity, the wheel, the vase of ambrosia, and the canopy and the parasol. The Taoist symbols are: a

religious influence

Buddhist symbols

flower-basket, the fan, castanets, the flute, and the magic wand. Mythical figures are also very common, as are moths, bats, butterflies and various floral motifs.

rug production   There are no exact records of when rug weaving began in China, but it has been suggested that the artform developed independently of any Persian influence, and most assuredly predates rug production in any other country. The earliest rugs known were distinguished by the use of very soft, almost sombre colors, including a subtle orange, blue, and brown. The current products from China are richer in coloration and more detailed. The Chinese rugs have an appearance distinct from any other carpets previously discussed. Their texture is one such feature. They are densely knotted, very thick, and frequently the pile *distinguishing features* is sculptured. The colors and motif selection also distinguish them from other carpets. Generally, the carpets produced today have an open field, with ornamentation in the center, sometimes at the sides and corners of the centerfield, and borders with solid bands surrounding one or sometimes two ornamented border stripes. The colors are also a distinguishing feature, especially the use of dark brown and black tones. These colors are extremely corrosive, causing wool fibers to disintegrate. Few Persian, Turkish or Turkoman products use these colors. The Chinese, however, have successfully incorporated them by using animal hair from yaks (which is dark brown or black), and from sheep with natural dark wool.

China has for centuries produced silk in abundance. Originally, it was raised only for the royal families and for the temples. The silk carpets produced can be classified into three general categories: (1)Those made entirely of silk, including the warp, weft and pile; (2) Those made with only a silk pile and woven on a stronger, but thicker cotton foundation; (3) Silk weave with silver and gold threads incorporated into the design.

silk rug types

The classification of Chinese carpets, like other rug-types, cannot be determined by virtue of the design alone. It is important to understand the various methods of manufacture, the materials, the colors, and the designs. All of these features combine to give a more accurate picture of the origin of a given carpet.

The materials used in the manufacture of Chinese rugs include silk, wool, cotton, and animal hair. The wool used in the pile is prepared in one of two ways, by hand spinning, or by machine spinning. Hand-spun wool is less uniform and will have some unevenness. Today, the fibers are produced by machine and only the antique rugs will reveal the less consistent feature of hand-spun wool. The silk threads today are also produced solely by machine. Animal hair, though not widely used for some time, was a typical feature of many Chinese carpets, and its popularity seems to be increasing as can be seen in the rugs exported today. It is difficult to distinguish immediately between wool and animal hair fibers. Under magnification, the

rug materials

wool & animal hair

fibers

animal hair will appear smooth, uniform and somewhat shiny, whereas wool yarn has small fibers protruding and is somewhat rough and dull.

The modern carpets exported from China today are available in various qualities, reflected in the density of their knots and in the process of manufacture. The lowest grade of carpets has a fabric backing attached so that the entire backside of the rug is covered. The rugs are produced in mass for export and are manufactured partially by mechanized process. They have fewer knots per square inch than the other grades, and are less durable. The other classes of rugs are made entirely by hand, and vary primarily in the knot density. The gauge used to measure knot density in Chinese rugs is by the number of knots per foot on the weft thread. For example, a 50 line rug, will have 50 knots woven onto a weft thread for every 12 inch section. This system is different from the knots per square inch used by most rug dealers for Persian and other Oriental carpets.

grades
of rugs

Types of Chinese rugs to follow:

Ning-Hsai
Tientsin
Samarkand

Ning-Hsai

Ning-Hsai is located on the upper Wang-Ho River near
the border of Mongolia. It has been famous for its wool
carpets which are produced in quantity today. The people
of the area are agriculturally oriented. They raise crops for
domestic consumption, livestock, and some cotton. They
have been influenced by the Mongolian styles as well as
by the Western Jesuit missionaries who established
missions in Ning-Hsai.

agriculture

The rugs were produced on crude vertical looms, usually
by both the men and women of the town. Traditionally,
the dyes, wool, and foundation threads were assembled by
the family members who then wove the rug. Small rugs,
ranging up to about six feet in length were the largest sizes,
but smaller items, including pillow covers, tent hangings,
saddle bags, and saddle blankets, were also made. These
carpets were not as densely knotted as the modern
Chinese carpets and the color range was limited to the
natural dyes available locally. The motifs were traditionally Chinese with round medallions, some dragon
forms, and Buddhist or Taoist symbols all sparingly ornamenting the centerfield. The borders usually mirrored
smaller versions of the motifs used in the center of the rug.

*early rug
production*

The modern carpets of Ning-Hsai are very similar to
Ning-Hsai antiques. However, they are no longer distinguished by the fine natural dyes of their 19th century

*modern
techniques*

open field

pieces. These rugs are available in larger sizes, and the designs still incorporate the traditional open field with Chinese symbols of good luck, longevity, and the Taoist or Buddhist symbols universally used throughout China.

ancient symbols

The religious motifs are by and large the most predominate symbols used in these rugs. Of the eight Buddhist symbols, the eight Taoist symbols and the mythical figures of folk history, the lotus, the magic wand and the knot of eternity are the most common. There are no specific design features that distinguish these rugs from others of Chinese origin.

colors

The antique rugs were made from natural dyes, and the spectrum included a delicate sky blue, a deeper shade closer to the evening sky, various shades of off-white to cream, peach, apricot, and a brilliant Chinese red. Today, the dyes are quality synthetics but the tones are brighter than the natural dyes of the antiques.

quick reference

1. Warp and Woof: Cotton.

2. Pile: Thick and somewhat long.

3. Sides: Overcast.

4. Ends: Fringed.

5. Sizes: Small to room-size carpets.

Tientsin

Tientsin is a major metropolitan center southeast of Peking. The rug industry is well organized and production has increased fifty percent in the last ten-year period. Factories have been built for materials processing and others for rug-weaving. The rug factories are the largest of their kind, where hundreds of workers are employed in each of a number of establishments.

increased production

The antique Tientsin carpets are usually of coarse wool or camel hair with fewer colors than the Peking rugs. Usually, three to four colors were used in one piece, and in most cases blue, black and brown tones predominated against an off-white background. Until the early 1900s, these were virtually the only colors used. Gradually, a growing export market developed and synthetic dyes were introduced. The color scale expanded then to include peach, yellow, red and green tones. The most common motifs employed were various forms of the rose.

limited colors

The modern rugs produced originate not only from the town of Tientsin, but from surrounding areas where rug cooperatives have been established. Production is geared for export, and though the wool is spun with the use of machines, the rugs themselves are produced entirely by hand. These rugs are made in sizes up to twenty feet in

rug cooperatives

length, and, like most other Chinese rugs, they can be specially ordered for size, color and design.

swastika motifs

Generally, the designs are conventional Chinese geometric motifs with various modifications of the swastika and the border of the Greek fret. Various forms of mythical animals and traditional floral forms are combined so that the modern rugs are more intricate, colorful, and dense than the antique products.

colors

The colors of Tientsin rugs are more limited than Peking rugs. They are almost always woven on an off white background with the most typical styles using a Chinese blue as the main color. Often these will be the only two colors, but other rugs, less common, will have two or more shades of blue, yellow, peach, and apricot.

quick reference

1. Warp and Woof: Always cotton.

2. Pile: Thick in modern, looser in antiques.

3. Sides: Overcast.

4. Ends: Fringed.

5. Sizes: Two feet square up to twenty feet in length.

Samarkand

Samarkand is located in Russia, somewhat more than one hundred miles east of Bokhara. The population consists of nomadic Turkomans, with Mongols and Chinese. The city is located on a branch of the Oxus River, and has served as a primary market and shipping port for textiles and other products of Chinese Turkestan. The Samarkand rugs are not produced in the city, but in outerlying areas, and are made predominately by nomad weavers.

*river
port*

Tamerlane, the Mongol conqueror, is buried in the city of Samarkand, which was a major center of learning. Tamerlane ordered that captured Persian artisans be brought to the city and teach the local weavers the techniques of Persian weaving. The earliest rugs made were extremely fine, silky and densely knotted with bright blue and red motifs. The patterns were geometric, generally large, and carefully executed. Persian influences can be seen in some of the floral motifs used in border ornamentation.

history

The modern rugs are not the quality products of one hundred years ago. The wools are not as silky and finely spun, and the knotting is looser. The pile is half as long again as the style followed years ago, but, with fewer knots per square inch, the modern rugs have proven to be far less durable than their predecessors.

*modern
rugs*

The field has large motifs, with a Turkoman flavor, but softened by Chinese sense of understatement of line. The

motifs

designs typically have from one to five central geometric medallions with the Chinese fret or wavy lines covering it and symmetrically scattered through it. Sometimes the dragon motif is used, and is surrounded by cloud bands in a circular form. Often a fretwork bordering the field is used.

border designs

The borders consist of coordinate stripes; sometimes the outer one is wider than the others and is finished with a band of solid colors. The inner border usually has the Greek meander pattern, and the outer border has floral patterns connected with the wavy lines typical of Persian border designs.

colors

These rugs are usually woven on a bright, red background with deep blue, cream, gray and orange highlights. Golden brown, soft fawn, and blue gray are other colors commonly used.

quick reference

1. Warp and Woof: Coarse cotton and sometimes wool.

2. Pile: Long, loosely knotted in the modern rugs.

3. Sides: Overcast or selvaged, sometimes in two colors.

4. Ends: Web and fringe.

5. Sizes: From three by six to nine by fifteen feet.

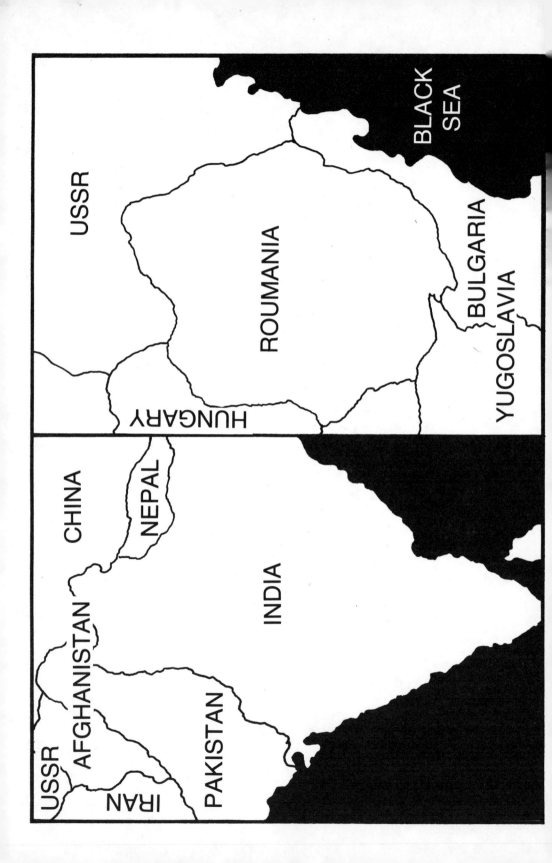

India
Pakistan
Roumania

Carpet production in India, Pakistan and Roumania has grown substantially in the last five years. These countries primarily make reproductions of traditional Persian, Caucasian, Turkoman and Chinese rugs. The products are hand knotted rugs using synthetic dyes and machine spun wool.

rug copies

Rugs produced in India are available in many styles. Chinese reproductions, Aubusson patterns and various Persian rug styles comprise India's major output. Many large department stores carry these rugs in sizes ranging up from two by three feet. There are varying qualities reflected in the diameter of the yarn used in weaving and the number of knots per square inch. The better quality rugs will have finer resolution of design, are more durable, and, as might be expected, are more expensive.

Indian rugs

Rug production is very well organized in Pakistan, and the industry has grown remarkably in the past five years. There are large factories producing hand made rugs in quantity. Tabriz, Sarouk, Kasak, and many Bokhara-style

Pakistani rugs

skillfully immitated

rugs are skillfully imitated. The rugs are produced to exact specifications, including the yarns, the knot density, the pattern, dyes, etc. The products must be identified as to country of origin and a tag appears on the back of the rug. It was true five years ago that significant savings could be had in purchasing Pakistani imitations of Persian and Caucasian rugs, but this does not seem to be always the case today. These rugs have become more costly.

Roumanian rugs

Within the last two years rug production has increased in Roumania. The carpets are manufactured by hand, and are made of good quality materials. The animal patterns of Tabriz are some of their better rugs, and though not as densely knotted as the Persian rugs, they are reasonably priced, durable, and attractive.

Indian Boy Weavers

Glossary

Afghanistan: Rug producing country. Herat, a famous Persian carpet center is now within its borders. Many nomadic tribes still produce rugs in Afghanistan. These rugs are marketed mainly as Afghan.

Angora: A long haired goat, and the hair used in many nomadic carpets, especially the products of Kurdistan.

Aniline: A synthetic dye introduced to the Oriental rug producing countries to replace the time-consuming procedures necessary in preparing natural dyes. They were subsequently outlawed in Persia and controlled in other rug-producing countries because they proved so unsatisfactory. Better synthetic dyes have since been developed. These are more permanent than the aniline dyes which were coal tar products.

Animal Forms: Not all Oriental rugs use animal motifs. Various forms are incorporated in some types of Persian, Chinese and Caucasian rugs. Birds, fish, horses, dragons and various domesticated animal forms have been the most frequently represented forms.

Apple Pattern: A design typical of Kurdistan, where it is highly stylized, and appears as an overall repeating pattern in the centerfield.

Ardebil: A name well known in reference to the famous mosque carpet discovered in Ardebil but produced in Kashan. The town is less distinguished for its own rugs.

Arshin: Persian increment of measurement, approximately equal to 30 inches, and used in reference to carpet dimensions.

Aubusson: Style of rug, French in character, usually in pastel rose, green, ivory and tan.

Azerbaijan: Persian rug-producing province.

Bakshaish: Mud-walled village east of Tabriz; carpets from this town were frequently marketed as Herez.

Barber Pole: Typically used as a border motif, incorporated in Faristan, Kabistan, Yomud and other Caucasian rugs.

Beluchistan: Rug producing district, rugs primarily made by nomadic weavers, usually in dark, somber red, blue and brown.

Bergamo: Ancient town north of Izmir in Turkey. An early stronghold of Christianity, ancient name was Pergamos (Pergamon).

Beshir: A term used to describe the web fringe end finish in Turkoman carpets.

Bibikabad: Center of carpet industry established near Hamadan, carpets marketed as Hamadan.

Bijapur: Indian city of carpet manufacture.

Bijar: Persian town northeast of Senneh and west of Teheran. Carpets produced primarily for export. The rugs are thick and dense, produced mostly by Kurdish weavers.

Bilooz: Term used to describe blue Bokhara rugs, more accurately rugs from Beluchistan.

Bird Forms: Various forms have been used in carpets throughout the Orient. Tabriz, Isfahan, and some Bokahara and Kasak rugs display these motifs.

Bokhara: Town located in the Caucasus. Carpets, saddle bags, and pillow covers are produced with the distinctive repeating geometric pattern called the 'gul'. Kilims, or woven rugs without nap, are also produced in this district.

Broussa: Ancient Ottoman capital where wool and silk carpets are produced.

Buckthorn: Plant used for dye making, it produces a Chinese green hue.

Burujird: A village located south of Hamadan, rugs woven here are marketed as Hamadan rugs.

Caesarea: Turkish town, center of rug production in the early 1900s, products generally of poor quality.

Camel Hair: Used extensively in rugs of the Hamadan district, typically the centerfield tan hue originated from the use of natural camel hair.

Campeche Wood: A natural source of red dye.

Carian Rugs: Another name for Meles rugs, or those originating from the coastal villages in Turkey.

Caucasian Rugs: Products of the Caucasus regions, now part of the Soviet Union.

Chaldea: Along with Babylonia, the ancient home of carpet weaving.

Chichi: Also spelled Tzitzi, carpets of the Caucasus, originating in the mountainous regions north of Daghestan, tribe of the same name.

China: One of the main centers of Oriental rug production, the products are distinguishable by thick piles, often with sculptured motifs and frequently open centerfields.

Chinese Motifs: Basically classified into three categories including the eight Taoist symbols, the eight Buddhist symbols, and mythical creatures such as dragon motifs.

Circassian Rugs: Also spelled Tcherkess, Chichi and Tzitzi. See Chichi above.

Coal Tar Dyes: Aniline dyes, first introduced in 1860 by European interests and promoted throughout Persia to replace the time consuming procedures necessitated in producing natural dyes. These aniline dyes were subsequently outlawed.

Cochineal: Variety of coccus insect which lives on oak trees in the Mediterranean regions. It is used to produce a rich carmine dye.

Color: Historically the use of color in rugs was dictated by its symbolic overtones. The Persian symbology is based on its religious history and so differs dramatically from that of the Chinese and other Oriental rug-producing cultures.

Cone: A pattern used in numerous Oriental carpets, sometimes called the pear or botah.

Cotton: Raised throughout the Orient, it is primarily used in the foundation threads of the carpet. Because of its durability, elasticity and natural immunity to moth damage, it is frequently preferred to wool for the foundation of a carpet.

Daghestan: Carpet-producing district in the Caucasus.

Demirjdi: Turkish rug producing town. Rug production began there around 1890. Rug production became a major industry within three years after a fire that devastated the town and left the inhabitants destitute. The products were thick and sometimes incorporated double and triple strands in the pile.

Derbend: Caucasian rug producing city, and major distribution point for rugs of the area.

Djushaghan: Another term for Josheghan rugs.

Dyes: Natural and synthetic sources used in rug production. Natural dyes are produced from animal, vegetable and mineral sources. Synthetic dyes are chemically produced.

Faristan: Province in southern Iran, major source of rug production.

Feraghan: Persian rug type and province.

Filik: Type of goat hair used in early rug production.

Fish Pattern: Also known as the Herati pattern.

Flame Pattern: Another name used for the Pear motif.

Floral Motifs: Both natural and stylized forms used throughout the Orient.

Flower of Henna: Another name for the Guli Hinnai motif.

Fretwork: Repeating geometric pattern universally used in rug design.

Gallnuts: Natural source for gray dye.

Geometric Designs: Used throughout the Orient, but particularly representative of Caucasian rugs.

Ghiordes: The Turkish knot form, also a rug of the same name.

Goat Hair: Used in the nap and foundation threads of some nomadic carpets.

Gorevan: Small village near Herez, rugs of the same name.

Grave Rugs: Also known as Turbehlik, derived from the word for grave. These carpets were traditionally made by family members to adorn the grave of the deceased.

Greek Cross: Motif used in Kasak and Chichi rugs.

Greek Key: Fret pattern.

Guli Hinnai: Same as the Flower of Henna motif. Typically the motif has a straight stem with three blossoms on either side.

Hamadan: Town in Iran where rugs are distributed. The rugs marketed as Hamadan are produced by a variety of groups spread around the town.

Hammamlik: A bath rug.

Hehbehlik: A saddle bag.

Herat: City now in Afghanistan, once a famous Persian carpet producing city.

Herati: Pattern named after the city of Herat, now used in many types of Persian rugs.

Herez: City north of Tabriz in Iran, rugs of the same name.

Isfahan: Town and center of carpet production in Iran.

Josheghan: Iranian town, center of carpet production, rug of the same name.

Kabistan: Caucasian rug type, also spelled Cabistan.

Kashkai: Tribe, and rug they produce.

Kasak: Caucasian rug type, and tribe.

Kermanshah: Iranian town located on the western border, rugs of the same name.

Kellegi: Rug, traditionally for head of the household, measuring four by five to five by ten feet.

Kermes: Insect used for red dye source.

Khorassan: Persian rug type and province.

Kilims: A flat woven rug, without knotted pile, produced in Iran, Turkestan and Turkey.

Kinari: Runner rugs.

Kirman: Old Persian province, town and rug of the same name.

Kir Shehr: Turkish rug producing town located in the Province of Konieh, rug of the same name.

Knots: The two most basic knot forms used throughout the Orient are the Persian and the Turkish knots, also termed Senneh and Ghiordes respectively.

Konieh: Turkish province, rugs of the same name.

Koultuk: Persian rug produced in the provinces of Ardelan and Irak Ajemi, resembling Kuba products, usually runners.

Kuba: A town located in the southeastern part of the Caucasian province of Daghestan.

Kulah: Turkish town and rug of the same name, rugs were made in predominately large sizes, and proved to be inferior carpets.

Kurdistan: Rug producing province, the nomadic people of the area are predominately Kurds, rugs are very thick, usually with long pile.

Kush: Wool shorn in Spring from bellies of sheep and goats, considered the finest wool.

Latch-Hook: Design used throughout Caucasian rugs and some Turkoman products.

Linen: Used as a foundation thread in some older carpets.

Looms: Horizontal and vertical, stationary and adjustable looms are the most common types used in Oriental rug manufacture.

Lotus: Floral ornament used in Chinese and Persian rugs.

Lule: Name of the old Persian fortified city, also used to refer to some Sarouk and Bijar rugs.

Madder: The root of rubia tinctorum, processed with alum and grape juice, to produce red dye.

Makatlik: Runner rugs.

Malgaran: Caucasian rug type.

Mecca: Holy city of the Moslems.

Medallions: Ornaments used in a variety of Oriental carpets, many varying forms, generally classified as either geometric or floral.

Meles: Turkish town and marketplace for the surrounding area, rugs of the same name are generally small, and somewhat coarse.

Meshed: Capital city of the Khorassan province in Iran, commercial center. Carpets of the same name, some with animal forms are woven with the Ghiordes knot.

Mina Khani: Persian floral motif, the flower patterns are joined by vines to form a rhomboid shape.

Mir: A motif also known as the Mir-i-botah or Seraband motif, having many forms, but always has a top hook shape, similar to a paisley design.

Mohammed: Founder of Islam who died in the seventh century AD.

Mosul: Ancient city in the center of Mesopotamia. Carpets of the same name, classed as Caucasian wares, have typical geometric patterns.

Namazlik: Prayer rugs.

Nomads: Rug weaving tribes that travel throughout Iran, Turkey and the Caucasus.

Odjaklik: Hearth rug, traditionally spread in front of the fireplace to honor a guest.

Ornament: Various forms used throughout the Orient, some of which are peculiar to specific rug types.

Oushak: Major rug-producing center in Turkey, carpets of the same name.

Oustri-Nan: Village near Hamadan, rugs produced in Oustri-Nan are marketed as Hamadan.

Palm: Motif also known as the Pear design.

Pergamos: Ancient name for the town of Bergamo.

Persia: Now Iran, the major source of Oriental carpets.

Persian Knot: Knot form, also known as the Senneh.

Pile: The nap formed when yarn is knotted around the foundation threads.

River Loop: Motif also called the Pear or Palm design.

Rochella: Lichen used for rich pink dye.

Rosette: Floral motif used in centerfield and border designs in many Persian and Caucasian rugs.

Royal Bokhara: Name loosely applied to the finest Bokhara rugs.

Russian Carpets: Rugs originating from the Caucasus regions.

Saffron: Natural source for yellow dye.

Saiga: A goat with yellow toned fleece, used in some Mongolian rugs.

Samarkand: Rugs and city of the same name.

Seraband: Rugs produced just south of Feraghan in Iran.

Sarouk: Famous Persian rug type.

Saw-Tooth: Typical motif in Kasak rugs.

Sedjadeh: Term translating as "floor covering," but usually referring to carpets seven feet long up to ten feet.

Senneh: Also known as the Persian knot, rug of the same name.

Selvage: A woven edge or end finish on a carpet.

Shah Abbas: Sixteenth century ruler of Persia.

Sheep Blood: Used for vermillion dye source.

Soumaki: Province west of Shirvan, now within the borders of Russia, also a term for Kashmir rugs.

Shiite: Islamic sect predominating in Iran. The shrine of the sect is located at Meshed.

Shiraz: Ancient capital city, carpet of the same name.

Shirvan: Caucasian rug type.

Silk: Fiber in rug production for foundation threads as well as in the pile.

Spinning: The process employed to form yarn for carpet manufacture, hand and machine spun yarn are currently used in modern rug making.

Star: Various forms used as motifs throughout the Orient.

Sultanabad: Carpet-producing center south of Hamadan.

Sumak: Plant root used for yellow dye source.

Sunnite Doctrine: Islamic cannon prohibiting the depiction of human or animal forms.

Swastika: Various forms used throughout the Orient in rug ornamentation.

Tabriz: Major city of commerce and rug production in Iran.

Tchechen: See Chichi.

Teheran: Present capital of Iran.

Tekke: Tribal name, weavers of the Bokhara rugs.

Transcaucasia: Region on the southern slopes of the Caucasus mountain range stretching to the northern border of Iran

Tree: Various forms used in rug ornamentation, the Tree of Life is the most common.

Trefoil: A reciprocal design used primarily in Caucasian products.

Turbehlik: Grave carpet.

Turkestan: Rug producing area now within the borders of Russia.

Turkish Knot: Knot form also known as the Ghiordes knot.

Turkoman: Rug classification including Bokhara (Tekke), Yomud, etc.

Tumeric: Natural substance used for yellow dye source.

Turunji: Term referring to medallion patterns which have curved outlines.

Tzoul: A fabric made from wool or goat hair.

Warp: Foundation threads on carpets which run the length of the rug.

Washed: A term used to describe a chemical treatment, or bath, used to bring out luster in dull, poor-quality wool.

Weave: The method in which a carpet is produced, varies as to knot forms, density of the knotting and the foundation of the rug.

Woof: Foundation threads on carpets which run the width of the rug.

Wool: The principal source of fibers for the pile in Oriental carpets.

Yomud: Tribe and rug of the same name.

Yuruk: Tribe related to the Kasaks, translates as mountaineer.

Zenjan: Old town on the road from Tabriz to Teheran.

Index

ISBN 0-89496-012-1

$7

There are numerous "coffee table" art books available that serve as a catalogue of some Oriental rugs. Although useful, most of these books tend to leave people confused and are more akin to a museum catalogue than serving as a useful working book for one intending to purchase or identify Oriental rugs.

Invaluable for both the prospective owner and experienced collector, the "Beginner's Guide To Oriental Rugs" presents clear illustrations of many of the most common designs found in Oriental rugs. Along with these designs are descriptions of the various rug makers that use the designs. To help refine things, the designs are followed by a detailed description of the rugs produced by each of the major rug producing tribes or towns. Complete advice is also given on evaluating a carpet, what makes one carpet more valuable than another, and how to take care of a carpet once you have it.

Other useful features include a glossary, maps of all major rug producing areas, the history of Oriental rugs and how the carpets are made, etc.. Here is the one book you will need to identify, evaluate and purchase Oriental rugs.